Swing Trading with Options

A Crash Course for Beginners to Trade Big Trends, Learn Best Strategies to Maximize Short Term Trading, Techniques to Trade Stocks, Options and Day Trading

Jim Douglas

clarifying purposes only and are the owned by the owners themselves, not affiliated with this document.

Table of Contents

Introduction to Swing Trading

In this first chapter, we are going to introduce the concept of swing trading. It's essential to distinguish swing trading from other common methods of trading and investing and you also need to know what the requirements for entry are. After introducing the concept of swing trading, we will explore how swing trading differs from day trading and also how it differs from long-term or buy and hold investing. We will also explore the question of who is best suited for swing trading. Before you start, you need to know if this is something that would be good for you and your financial situation. We will do that in the chapter with a discussion of the tax implications of swing trading.

What is swing trading?

The concept of swing trading is deceptively simple. All it means is that you buy and sell stocks or other investments to make short-term profits. In other words, swing trading seeks to profit from short-term price movements on the stock market (or other markets such as currency trading). However, unlike day trading, the price movements we are interested in last from days to weeks or possibly up to a couple of months or so.

It differs from day trading in one key aspect. Swing trading involves holding securities overnight, possibly for weeks at a time. Therefore, you can be looking for short-term swings in the price of a stock, for example. However, you aren't looking for that swing in price to occur over the course of a single day, but rather over a few days, or weeks. Some people who swing trade can even lengthen that time period out to a couple of months or so. You might even say you are a swing trader if your strategy is to hold stocks for several months, but buy low and sell high over that period.

As you might guess, the level of involvement and stress in swing trading is lower than what you would find with day trading. We are going to explore the differences between swing trading and day trading in detail in a later section. Nevertheless, generally speaking, it's going to involve less upfront capital and a lower level of involvement in the daily movements of stocks or whatever market you are involved with. Swing trading can be used on stocks, Forex, commodities, and even with crypto currencies. However, for the purposes of this book, we will generally focus on the stock market. The principles are the same no matter what you trade.

Where can you use swing trading?

Swing trading can be used in virtually any market. It's a technique, rather than something specialized for a specific market like crypto currency. Nevertheless, swing traders primarily trade on stock markets. But you can use swing trading as a technique when trading commodities, currencies, and anything else that will see price swings up-and-down over the time periods of interest, and that means you could apply swing trading to anything that gets traded. You could even think of trading options as a form of swing trading since you're hoping to profit on the same moves of the stock, although options are quite a different ball game overall. Our focus in this book is going to be on stock trading. But keep in mind that you could use the exact same techniques, including the methods of analysis for the most part on currency markets as well.

Chapter 1:
Swing Trading Vs Other Trading Styles

Day Trading

So you're thinking about making the jump from swing trading to day trading. You've had relative success with swing trading for a while, and you want to cash in on working the market full time. But the important question is: Can you make a living off of day trading? And further: Can it be sustainable, despite market fluctuations?

There are a lot of informal investors and swing brokers out there, a large number of them taking part in the securities exchange at various levels. A few people use day exchanging professionally, time others simply exchange for a couple of hours daily to get some additional salary. One of the inquiries I get posed to a ton is, "when is the perfect time to make the jump to full-time day exchanging?"

Obviously, there is no general response to this inquiry, anyway there are a couple of contemplations that become an integral factor. It ought to be noticed that day exchanging isn't as impressive as it is frequently depicted to be. Exchanging stocks isn't tied in with "making bank" or carrying on with an extraordinary way of life. For full-time informal investors, exchanging stocks is a profession. This implies it requires work – work that involves sitting by the PC for quite a long time multi day gazing at screens. You are not ensured to make a huge number of dollars. Hell, you're not ensured to get paid. Day exchanging is one of only a handful couple of vocation decisions where you are not ensured a check, and you may even lose cash in the wake of contributing hours of your time.

Disheartened at this point? Try not to be. This isn't expected to scrutinize day exchanging as a profession. I exchange each day and I cherish it. This post is proposed to be a rude awakening that enables you to set reasonable desires that will enable you to find a way to accomplish your objectives. It's likewise imperative to take note of that this post is focused towards individuals who need to realize how to begin day exchanging full-time (which means you are leaving your other activity to seek after day exchanging full-time). A portion of these focuses won't be applicable to the individuals who exchange as an extracurricular movement.

Day Trading for a Living - A Few Necessary Pre-Requisites

Preparing – Before you significantly consider taking the jump towards turning into a full-time stock broker, you should ensure you are appropriately prepared. You wouldn't leave your place of employment to turn into an architect with no appropriate preparing, isn't that so? What are your of odds of succeeding? A similar rationale applies to exchanging. Begin building up the correct ability before considering a vocation in day exchanging. We have an assortment of free and paid assets to kick you off on your voyage.

Experience – You can peruse 1000 books on exchanging hypothesis and still get squashed by the business sectors. Hypothesis and practice are two distinctive ranges of abilities. Most brokers need to invest some energy really exchanging before they can get a genuine vibe for the business sectors.

Consistency – If you are notwithstanding thinking about turning into a full-time dealer, ensure you are exchanging reliably. This will enable you to set sensible desires for what's to come. Consistency is evidence that you have really built up a pertinent range of abilities. For another merchant, there's increasingly long haul an incentive in making $5,000/month for a year than making $200,000 your first month and $0 the remainder of the year. Certainly, one gives a higher transient fiscal worth, be that as it may, it is less economical over the long haul.

There is no "enchantment number" with regards to computing the measure of experience required. Various dealers will learn at various paces. One merchant might almost certainly wind up reliable in a year, while others may take a couple of years. It's critical to consider these next couple of contemplations.

Step by step instructions to Become a Day Trader Full-Time

Both day exchanging and increasingly traditional profession ways have their advantages. A traditional activity promises you a pay (and, some of the time, benefits), though day exchanging has higher hypothetical versatility and enables you to work for yourself. For most full-time informal investors, the greatest advantage is that you get the opportunity to do what you cherish at a vocation that reliably challenges you. Sound engaging? Consider the accompanying:

As a full-time informal investor, you will have less soundness, particularly as you begin. You will have great months, terrible months, extraordinary months, and rationally debilitating months. While this crazy ride of feelings is a piece of what makes day exchanging energizing, it can likewise be unpleasant whenever drawn closer inappropriately.

Monetary Considerations

Record for Your Day Trader Salary and Build a Safety Net

Exiting your profession means leaving your ensured salary stream. An informal investor's compensation is never ensured. Indeed, exiting your profession implies you get the opportunity to get away from the dullness of a 9-to-5, however in the event that you need to day exchange professionally, you should be set up for what pursues. Make a monetary arrangement.

You should set aside up enough cash to cover your costs for a long time. This will remove a portion of the worry from exchanging. In case you're not exchanging to pay the lease, you can settle on a lot more brilliant choices. Obviously, this methodology depends vigorously on your capacity to precisely compute this number. It's smarter to overestimate than disparage.

Make a point to represent everything, including:

Lease, Utilities, Sustenance, Toiletries, PDA bills, Protection, Excitement And so forth

Try not to undercut yourself here. It might be anything but difficult to state, "I can live without excitement for a long time" until you are 2 months into gazing at the screens for 12 hours every day. Be practical, be exact, and plan appropriately.

On the off chance that your determined spending plan is $3000/month, set aside $72,000 and adhere to your financial limit. In the event that you can live off of $2000/month, set aside $48,000 for costs. This spending will differ impressively by individual yet the ultimate objective is the equivalent. You are covering your costs for the following couple of years with the goal that you can withdraw yourself from money related pressure and have the absolute best at progress.

Your Stock Trading Account

We talked about the significance of setting aside up enough cash to cover your costs. You will likewise need the money to support a record. By and by, the measure of cash vital will fluctuate by individual. You will require in any event $25,000 to day exchange routinely (in view of the Pattern Day Trader rule), anyway you can swing exchange with less. Pick a number and arrangement the records.

Picking a number is tied in with giving yourself the most obvious opportunity. Evaluating a record too soon before learning consistency is just going to put yourself at the danger of losing all the quicker. Beginning little cutoff points what you can do yet in addition restricts your hazard versus beginning bigger. Remember, that your business ledger and money market fund are totally independent. You shouldn't need to destroy from your business ledger to take care of your exchanging expenses and you shouldn't need to dismantle from your exchanging record to cover costs.

Different Considerations

Opportunity Cost

As yet, we examined the money related arranging associated with taking a jump into full-time exchanging. It's likewise essential to concentrate on the open door cost of the jump. What are you surrendering by making the change?

For instance, on the off chance that you are making $100,000/year + benefits at your other activity, you are leaving a strong compensation and entering a vocation with an erratic pay. Will you have the option to find a comparable line of work following 2 years if exchanging doesn't go as arranged? Perhaps indeed, perhaps no. Make a point to represent this before focusing on the jump.

Character Traits

When you become a full-time broker, you enter a universe of 100% responsibility. No one is causing you to get up each morning and nobody is instructing all of you day. You are the driver of your own salary and you are the one in particular who considerations enough to produce it. Ensure you have the control and legitimate hierarchical aptitudes important to capitalize on this procedure. Is it accurate to say that you are somebody who appreciates the self-rule of working for yourself or do you lean toward being determined what to do? It is safe to say that you are ready to hold yourself under tight restraints and adhere to a calendar or do you veer off and do your own thing? Do you need solidness or does hazard keep the business sectors energizing? Be set up for the way of life change similarly as you are set up for the money related changes.

Day exchanging stocks is an inconceivably remunerating profession way with a considerable rundown of advantages and advantages. This post was intended to help individuals get ready for the progress. The prizes of day exchanging professionally can be energizing, making a few people overlook the work associated with arriving. Give this present to you a chance to practical and help you adopt a sensible strategy to the change. Arrangement is critical. You can arrive on the off chance that you make the essential strides.

Most significant is to appreciate doing it, for the cash as well as to discover some new information regular and not to feel debilitated by absence of learning or age.

Progressions in innovation have guaranteed anybody with a working web association can begin day exchanging professionally. Be that as it may, while it may be conceivable, how simple is it and how on earth do you approach doing it? This page will take a gander at the advantages of day exchanging professionally, what and where individuals are exchanging, in addition to offer you some significant hints.

Is Day Trading For A Living Possible?

The principal thing to note is indeed, bringing home the bacon on day exchanging is a superbly reasonable vocation, yet it's not really simpler or less work than an ordinary daytime work.

The advantages are fairly that you work for yourself, and can design your work hours any way you need. Exchanging on a workstation likewise implies you can do it anyplace, whenever.

Be careful – there are numerous out there who guarantee to make a fortune on day exchanging, however generally these individuals are attempting to sell you something. Try not to accept the promotion or that there is such a mind-bending concept as "pain free income".

There are approaches to make it simpler however – for instance, you don't have to make to such an extent on the off chance that you live in (or move to) a minimal effort, low-charge nation. Eliminating living expenses can likewise have a major effect, as "bringing home the bacon" on something generally implies that pay spreads costs.

Advantages versus Drawbacks

Regardless of the trouble, there are some undeniable advantages to day exchanging professionally. To give some examples:

No supervisor – You're your own manager. No all the more pandering to the necessities of requesting and outlandish managers. You can work decisively the manner in which you need.

Hours – You set your own working hours. In this day and age there is consistently a market open. In this way, you can pick when you need to work and for to what extent, fitting it around different duties. In the event that you need a multi week occasion, there's no HR division to explore first.

Overheads – No progressively costly train ticket to get the chance to work. No more petroleum and stopping costs. Not any more expensive suits. You essentially need a PC, a web association and some funding to get moving.

Solace – Whilst every other person is pressing their shirt for the day ahead, you can slip into some comfortable garments and start your 15-foot drive to your work area, with a crisp mug of espresso. Not any more stuffy office or diverting partners to manage. You work from the solace of your own home.

Downsides

In spite of the conspicuous appeals, remarks about day exchanging professionally likewise feature a few drawbacks. The most predominant of which are:

Lone way of life – Your associates may have driven you up the divider now and again, however now and then it's consoling to have individuals around. Day exchanging professionally can get forlorn. On the off chance that you don't care for being individually, reconsider.

Conflicting pay – Your pay will vacillate enormously. You may make $3,000 one day and after that lose $2,500 the following. You likely won't have a steady compensation to depend on. What's more, in the event that you take a vacation day work you, you won't get paid a penny.

Profession movement – The main thing that can improve is your takings. You may likewise think that it's difficult to get again into the business world. Some time or another exchanging professionally discussions have proposed you'll be less employable by the end.

The fight against bots – Algorithms, computerized frameworks, and bots are on the whole assuming control over the market. They are presently in charge of a gigantic 60% of all market volume. While, there will consistently be a spot for people in the market, you'll have to discover better approaches to adjust and advance in the event that you need to keep up an edge.

Long-Term Investments

Position traders seek to hold an asset for a long period of time, but they are not buy and hold investors. They are traders who seek to earn profit from their trades, rather than holding assets in order to build wealth. Position traders on the stock market can hold positions for several weeks, months, or even years.

Position trading on the stock market can be viewed as a long-term version of swing trading. They will rely on both fundamental and technical analysis. Since position traders will on average hold assets for a longer time period than a swing trader, fundamental analysis plays a larger role in their decision making. Capital is more liquid for swing traders, since they are entering and exiting trades more often. Position traders will have their capital locked up in an asset. This can last for potentially long periods. Since they are holding long-term positions, position traders are more sensitive to economic trends and the overall state of the stock market.

Position trading is not an active form of trading. They are hoping the long-term appreciation of the asset will lead to profits. Day traders may do hundreds of trades per year, but position traders enter into about 10-12 trades per year on average. Swing traders are more concerned with short term fluctuations in asset price than position traders, although position traders need to be alert to trend reversals that could cause losses.

There are many similarities between swing trading and position trading. They both rely on fundamental and technical analysis, and compared to day traders hold their positions longer. They are both trend followers who seek the right entry and exit points for their trades. Overall, it's simply a matter of trading frequency.

While options are a perfect fit for swing traders, position traders won't trade weekly or monthly options. However, you can use LEAPS for position trading, since you can hold them for long time periods, even up to two years.

Position trading is also a popular Forex strategy. Fundamental analysis plays an important role in Forex position trading, even including macroeconomic factors like changes in GDP. They will use technical analysis to determine entry and exit points for trades. Position traders also have a wider stop loss, which may require more up front capital. However, position trading on Forex tends to have a favorable risk-to-reward ratio.

Swing Trading

Swing trading is a type of forex trading that endeavors to profit on a stock or any budgetary instrument over a time of a couple of days to half a month. Swing brokers fundamentally utilize specialized investigation to search for foreign currency trading openings. These merchants may use basic investigation notwithstanding examining value patterns and examples.

The objective of swing exchanging is to catch a lump of a potential value move. While a few dealers search out unpredictable stocks with bunches of development, others may lean toward increasingly quiet stocks. In either case, swing exchanging is the way toward recognizing where an advantage's cost is probably going to move straight away, entering a position, and after that catching a lump of the benefit from that action. Swing trading includes holding a position either long or short for more than one exchanging session, yet for the most part not longer than half a month or two or three months. This is a general time allotment, as certain exchanges may last longer than several months, yet the merchant may at present think of them as swing exchanges.

Effective swing dealers are just hoping to catch a lump of the normal value move, and after that proceed onward to the following chance.

Many swing brokers evaluate exchanges on a hazard/remunerate premise. By investigating the outline of a benefit, they figure out where they will enter, where they will put a stop misfortune, and after that foresee where they can get out with a benefit. On the off chance that they are gambling $3 per share on an arrangement that could sensibly create an $8 gain, that is a great risk and reward. Then again, gambling $10 to make $10 or just make $6 is not as positive.

Swing dealers will regularly search for circumstances on the day by day graphs, and may watch 1-hour or 15-minute diagrams to discover exact entry and stop loss positions. Swing merchants fundamentally utilize specialized examination, because of the transient idea of the exchanges. All things considered, crucial investigation can be utilized to upgrade the examination. For instance, if a swing merchant sees a bullish arrangement in a stock, they might need to confirm that the essentials of the benefit look positive or are increasing progressively.

There are a number of advantages to swing trading as a way of making good profits over a definite period of time;

• It expands the transient benefit potential by catching the greater part of market swings.

Swing Trading with Options

• It needs a shorter time to exchange than day trading.

• The merchants can depend only on specialized examination, improving the exchanging procedure.

Despite the advantages, there are a number of disadvantages of swing trading that any trader must consider;

• Swing traders regularly miss longer-term inclines for momentary market moves.

• Unexpected market inversions can result in significant misfortunes.

• Exchange positions are liable to medium-term and end of the week market chance.

This text is meant for anybody who wants to supplement their income and find an alternative income stream that is convenient for them. Swing trading can be done right from home, you do not have to report to an office or be subjected to a single boss.

When you start swing trading, you will develop a specific routine that will allow you to maximize on your knowledge of the stock market and make a profit as a result. The contents of this text target almost any individual who is ready to start a second job that they have full control over. Similarly, this text is also useful for anybody looking to quit their current profession and start a new one. Since you will be working from the comfort of your home, it is a good way to start over your career and pursue something you actually enjoy doing.

There are no restrictions over who can start swing trading; doctors, politicians, bankers and even chefs have quit their day time jobs to start swing trading. As much as there are disadvantages associated with this kind of venture, almost anybody can start it and achieve success within a short time.

All in all, swing trading has become very popular in the world for a number of reasons;

Since you do not need to lounge around for quite a long time and years, for example, long haul contributing, you will know how a lot of cash you have made on your exchanges and the amount of that you can remove from your speculation account as pay. You can boost the sum you procure from doing as meager as three to five exchanges for every week that ordinarily are acknowledged and completed in under ten days. Swing trading is extremely specialized in nature and dependent on after searching for transient patterns where stocks increment in worth rapidly. As indicated by various forex merchants, swing exchanging time periods enable you to concentrate on the center market development and recognize pattern energy effectively. It just takes two or three seconds to get your predisposition on a swing exchanging time period.

You do not need to get into a wide assortment of information regions, for example, organization monetary records and different things so as to get the required data to make an exchange. This increasingly thin spotlight encourages you focus on a couple of key territories that you will turn out to be generally excellent at. It is about simply the cost and patterns when swing exchanging. This reality likewise will in general make swing exchanging significantly less distressing than other momentary exchanging styles, for example, day trading.

Maybe the most noteworthy favorable position of swing exchanging is its capacity to limit hazard. As indicated by prevalent swing brokers, stop misfortunes are regularly littler than longer term exchanges. This takes into account you to put bigger estimated positions rather than incredibly low utilized ones by means of the more extended term patterns. Another factor in the decrease of hazard is you are for the most part making just three to five exchanges every week so you don't have this wide range of speculations to mind; it enables you to keep extremely close track on your exchanges requiring just a short measure of time.

As was expressed, swing exchanging more often than not includes exchanges that are over with in only a couple of days as of recently. You will know how fruitful your system has been in many cases in under seven days. This enables you to have the option to always change your swing exchanging technique until you have it to the point where it is continually winning you cash. It is the sort of exchanging that does not need to be always checked so it is useful for speculators who do not have a great deal of time, for example, the individuals who exchange on low maintenance premise while holding down another all-day work. When an individual has turned out to be capable at specialized examination, again in accordance with the limited focal point of things you are taking a gander at about a stock, it does not set aside a ton of effort to distinguish the key patterns and make your exchanges.

Types of Analysis used in Swing Trading

Candlesticks

A candlestick is a marking on a stock chart or graph that represents the following four data points:

- Open
- High

- Low
- Close

Candlesticks are colored red or green on a chart. Just for the sake of seeing a representation, here is a screenshot of a couple of candlesticks for a specific stock:

Candlesticks can be green or red in color. The rectangle shown on the chart is the body of the candlestick. If the candlestick is green, the bottom represents the opening price, and the top represents the closing price. The narrow lines emanating from the candlestick body are called the wicks. If the candlestick is green color, that means the price of the stock went up over the given time period. If you have a monthly chart, then the green color indicates that by the close of the day, for that day the stock went up in price.

A red candlestick indicates that the price of the stock went up for the period of measurement. If the time period is one month, then the top indicates the opening price, while the bottom of the body indicates the opening price.

Different time periods can be illustrated on a graph. In many cases, we are interested in short term price changes for day trading. We can look at a chart that shows whether the price went up or down over a five-minute period. If the price went up over the five-minute periods, the candlestick is green in color. The top of the candlestick body indicates the price at the end of the five-minute period. The bottom indicates the price at the start of the five-minute period.

On the other hand, if the candlestick is colored red, over the given five-minute period, the top represents the price at the start of the five minute period, while the bottom of the body represents the price at the end of the vie minute period.

Reversals

A reversal is a major change in the direction of the price of the stock. So, the trend completely shifts and moves in the opposite direction. In order to look for reversals, look at the candlesticks on a stock market chart. The body of the candlesticks and its size relative to the previous (to the left) candlesticks is what is important. First, let's consider a signal for a reversal where a declining stock price is going to be going up in the future. If the candlestick of the most recent time is larger and fully engulfs or covers the candlestick to the left, and it's the opposite color, i.e. a green candlestick following red candlesticks, this indicates a reversal of a downtrend into an increasing stock price. This is a good time to go long or buy calls.

On the other hand, let's now consider the case where the stock price is going up, with multiple green candlesticks in a row. Then it is followed by an engulfing red candlestick. This indicates a reversal so we will expect the stock price to begin going down. That is, this is a point where we should short the stock, or if trading options invest in puts.

The larger the engulfing candlestick, the stronger the reversal signal is. That indicates that the change in direction has a significant conviction behind the reversal, which is the confidence of investors, larger volume and the price will change in larger amounts over short time periods. If the wicks engulf the wicks of the previous period that is an even stronger signal that a reversal is underway.

When using reversals as a trading strategy, you need a minimum of five candlesticks in a five-minute chart. Then look at the relative strength index, which helps you evaluate overbought or oversold stocks. The RSI ranges from 0-100. At the top of an uptrend, if the RSI is above 90 that indicates that the stock is overbought and is probably going to be heading into a downturn. On the other hand, if you are looking at the bottom of a downturn, if the RSI is 10 or below, this indicates that the stock is oversold. That could be a signal that is about to see a price increase.

When looking for reversals, indecision candlesticks can be important in combination with the other variables discussed here. An indecision candlestick indicates either an upturn or a downturn. That is if you see a downturn followed by several indecision candlesticks, that could mean that the stock is about to turn upward again. Or vice versa – if an upturn is followed by several indecision candlesticks, that can indicate a reversal resulting in a downward trending stock price.

Looking at the wicks can be important as well. When the lower wick of the candlestick is longer, that may indicate that the price dropped over the period of the candlestick, but the stock turned and was bought up. On the other hand, if the candlestick has a long wick at the top that may indicate that the stock was bid up too much over the period. Traders lost interest and began selling off the stock. At any time there appears to be a reversal, a trend of indecision candles or stagnation represents a buying opportunity no matter which direction the stock may be trending. That is if you are in the midst of a downturn and the stock is moving sideways, then it may be a good time to go long on it or buy calls. The opposite is true if the stock is at the top of a potential reversal. If it's moving sideways, it may be a good time to invest in puts. Keep in mind that this does not always work. The best indicator is whether or not a green (red) candlestick following a red (green) candlestick which engulfs the candlestick to the left is the best indicator of a coming reversal.

The Bull Flag

A bull flag is a strong upward trend in the stock. However, after shooting upward, the stock enters a phase of consolidation, when people slow down or stop buying, but before a new rise may begin. The "flag pole" is a steep rise in the price of the stock over a very short time period. The "flag" is a time period when the price is high but stays about the same. A bull flag is a symbol of a buying opportunity for a stock that has already shown a significant increase. You should set your desired profit, buy and then sell when it begins increasing again up to the point where you have set to take your profit. You should always include a stop-loss, a bull flag is no guarantee and the price might actually start dropping.

When there is a bull flag, it is bordered along the bottom by a level below which the stock is not dropping, known as the support. On the top, there is a level above which the stock is not rising. This is called resistance. Eventually, the stock is going to break out of the resistance so you want to buy before this happens, as the stock may see a rapid rise again. A bull flag may occur multiple times during the day as the stock trends upward.

Bollinger Bands

Bollinger bands are a very popular indicator for day traders, looking for price actions and indicators for strengthening or weakening. These were developed by none other than John Bollinger. Bollinger bands are adaptive trading bands. A trading band is simply a range of prices for security (aka stock). In particular, Bollinger bands represent:

• Volatility

• The extent of price movement

• They indicate trend lines defining support and resistance

Bollinger bands are calculated using standard deviation. However, you don't need to be an expert in statistics to understand how Bollinger bands are calculated or what they represent. In short, a Bollinger band is calculated relative to some average of prices, for example, the moving average over a given number of periods. What the Bollinger band represents then, is the spread of prices about that average.

Bollinger bands only measure closing prices and how to spread out they are. Typically, they measure the 20 periods moving average, but they can be used for 50 or 100 periods.

Bollinger bands are dynamic. You will see them around the candlesticks in a stock chart. When they narrow, that is known as a volatility squeeze. If they spread out, that is a volatility spread.

• If the bands are narrow that indicates that the prices over that period are falling within a smaller range (i.e. the closing prices for each period are relatively similar to each other).

• If the bands are wider, that indicates a greater spread in prices, that is individual prices differ from each other a lot more – put another way, there is more volatility.

What signals are there with Bollinger bands that a day trader can look for?

• If wick of a candlestick at the bottom hits the Bollinger band, that can be taken as a buy signal. The stock is oversold, so it's a good time to buy.

• When the candlestick touches or crosses the upper Bollinger band, then the stock is overbought.

Of course, the vice versa applies, if a candle hits the top band, it may not be a sell signal, you may want to short or buy puts.

When the candlesticks are hitting the Bollinger bands, this may indicate a reversal. A hammer at the bottom of a reversal touching the bottom Bollinger band is a nice buy signal in many cases. Reversal candlesticks that touch a Bollinger band are a solid indicator that there is really a reversal coming.

In the opposite direction, if you are looking to short a stock or invest in puts, then you want to look for shooting stars that touch the upper Bollinger band. This can indicate a reversal or a coming downturn. If you are long on a stock and this condition arises, that indicates that it is a good time to sell.

When using Bollinger bands, you will want to look at the shape of the candlestick itself. This can strengthen or weaken your indicators. If you see a hammer at the bottom of the Bollinger bands, this can indicate a coming upturn in the stock so it's a good time to go long. On the other hand, if you see a shooting star touching the top Bollinger band, that may be an indicator that it is either a good time to sell or a good time to short or buy puts. Using Bollinger bands is not going to be a perfect indicator, but you can combine your observations about the shapes of the candlesticks and whether or not they are shooting stars or hammers together with the Bollinger bands to get a reasonable conjecture as to whether the stock is likely to move in one direction or in the opposite direction. In other words, looking at the candlesticks together with their relationship to the Bollinger bands will help you determine whether or not a given stock is primed to reverse.

Fading

Fading is a bet against dumb money in the stock market. The technique is based on shorting stocks that have moved upward rapidly, typically in the first hour after market open. The idea is based on the belief that the stock is overbought that is retail investors have jumped in on stock and bid up to the price based on some news about the stock. During the process, eager retail investors will bid the price up beyond its intrinsic value, so as the trading day goes on the price will begin dropping.

The point to get in and short the stock is to look for when the upswing begins slowing down or fading. Obviously, fading is a high-risk strategy, you don't have the same information available as the institutional investors so may be guessing wrong even when it appears that the rise of the stock is sputtering. You should always protect yourself with a stop-loss.

Technical Analysis

Fundamental analysis is important, and it plays a central role in the analysis of buy-and-hold and dividend investors. It's also important for swing traders to determine the health of a company you are thinking of investing in. However, the main tools of trade for the swing trader center around technical analysis and reading charts. Over the course of days, you are interested in spotting trends, changes to trends, and price boundaries for stocks. There are several tools used to do this but one of the most important tools in the industry goes by the name "candlesticks". These are colored markers on stock charts, and they can be displayed for any time frame of interest. For example a day trader may look at 1 minute, 5 minute, 1 hour, or 4 hour candlesticks. As a swing trader you're probably more interested in looking at daily candlesticks and then following trends as they develop over days and weeks.

In either case, candlesticks work the same and the same rules apply. Please note that while we will often refer to "stock" in our discussion, candlesticks are used in any investment context such as with Forex.

Swing traders are going to make money on price swings, as the name implies. Trading strong trends is one way that swing traders can handsomely profit. However, you can also profit when a security is trading in a range of prices that is bouncing up and down between two price levels and not seeming able to break out. Profits are still to be made as the price fluctuates up and down, although you may be making larger profits when trading trends. In fact most swing traders look to trade trends for this reason. Some traders will do both, trading ranges as a matter of course and trading trends when the opportunities present themselves. In this chapter we are going to look at some tools that help you spot reversals, which are important for looking at entry and exit points for a trade.

Fundamental Analysis

Fundamental analysis is a process by which you study the fundamentals behind a financial asset. On the Forex markets, you will be looking at the state of the economy, GDP growth, and political factors that impact the overall picture and stability of the country. If these items are looking good, that means the currency for that country will gain strength. But since currencies are traded in pairs on Forex, that means you also have to compare fundamentals between countries. If Europe looks strong but Japan is looking even better, then the Japanese Yen would strengthen as compared to the Euro.

When it comes to stocks and options, the fundamentals include profit margins, price to earnings ratios, cash flow and other indicators that give a picture of the overall health and prospects of the company. You'll be wanting to take a look at quarterly earnings, and reviewing earnings calls for companies that you are invested in. Fundamental analysis also means looking for stocks that are currently undervalued. The price of undervalued stocks is likely to increase at some point in the future, so spotting an undervalued stock could be useful for the swing trader.

Since swing traders have different time horizons as compared to buy and hold investors, short-term results like earnings calls are going to take on a larger role, as compared to looking at trends in revenue and profits over the course of years. A good earnings call can send prices soaring, while failing to meet expectations can send stocks into a rapid decline. When there are events like this as a swing trader you have to be ready to seize upon them as quickly as possible.

It's also important to keep your eye on company news of a more general nature. If a product fails or ends up creating legal trouble for a company that can be an opportunity to short the stock or invest in put options. Alternatively, the release of a new product that exceeds expectations can be an opportunity to go long on the stock.

Behavioral Economics

It would be best for you to develop an execution checklist. Note: this is not your entire trading strategy as we'll see in later chapters but merely the checklist you follow prior to placing an order. It could be as follows:

• Is price in a trend or range? Or can't say?

• How strong is the trend (if in a trend)? How defined/clean is the range (if in a range)? Assign a number on the scale if using one.

• Is this number something I'm comfortable with to participate further?

• If so, what are my trend strategies (if in a trend)? What are my range strategies (if in a range)?

• Execute.

Again, this is easy to write down but difficult to execute because of the highly charged trading environment newbies partake in. The mental aspect of trading is an important skill you must master if you are to succeed. This is addressed in later chapters. For now, just remember what was said earlier about the ideal trading state being one of slightly bored attachment. If you are not in this state, then do not trade.

When to and When Not to

At this point, it would serve us well to list out a few do's and don'ts of trading.

Do not trade if:

• Your state is one of over excitement or action seeking.

• Your state is depressed, sad or overwhelmed.

• You feel hurried or rushed and feel like there's too much going on and can't keep up.

• You want to make money in a hurry and NOW!

• You think you've found the ultimate strategy which unlocks all market secrets.

• You're dreaming of luxury cars and mansions and total financial independence.

Do trade if:

• You recognize how much more you need to learn and are determined to put in the work.

• You know you are willing and ready to step aside and admit "I don't know."

• You are risking only what you can afford to lose as capital.

• You are realistic about your money goals. The world's biggest hedge funds consider a 15% annual return a brilliant performance. You're OK with producing this much amount of money from your trading.

This chapter has strayed a bit beyond the technical aspects of trading and into the mindset and risk portion of your trading skills. We will look at this in later chapters in more detail. For now, you must understand that your trading success depends on much more than just your technical strategy. You need to master risk management as well as your mindset. Ideally, you will start working on your mindset first, then your risk management and then finally on your technical strategy. With most people though, this is reversed. This is OK as long as you work on all aspects and not just the technical portion, expecting some secret to be unlocked via some unknown indicator. You might as well learn now that no such thing exists. Never has and never will.

Successful traders make money via mastery in all three aspects of trading: Technical Skills, Mindset and Risk Management. It behooves you to master all aspects of all three. Now with that little warning, it is time to delve into the individual indicators and strategies you can use with them as part of your technical plan to trade. Remember, each indicator detailed in the next few chapters is meant to be used in certain environments and in some cases, well defined environments. They're great tools but they need to be used appropriately. No one ever built a cabinet using a hammer to drive screws after all.Swing Trading Pros and Cons

Swing Trading with Options

Swing trading options are gets that give the carrier the right, yet not the commitment, to either purchase or sell a measure of some basic resource at a pre-decided cost at or before the agreement lapses. Options can be obtained like most other resource classes with financier venture accounts.

Options are amazing in light of the fact that they can upgrade a person's portfolio. They do this through included pay, assurance, and even influence. Contingent upon the circumstance, there is normally an alternative situation fitting for a financial specialist's objective. A prominent model would utilize choices as a successful fence against a declining securities exchange to restrict drawback misfortunes. Alternatives can likewise be utilized to create repeating pay. Moreover, they are regularly utilized for theoretical purposes, for example, betting on the bearing of a stock. There is nothing free with stocks and bonds and options are the same. They include certain dangers that the financial specialist must know about before making an exchange.

Swing Trading Stocks; Pros and Cons

A stock or share, otherwise called an organization's value is a budgetary instrument that speaks to possession in an organization or company and speaks to a proportionate case on its benefits (what it claims) and income (what it creates in benefits).

Stock proprietorship suggests that the investor claims a cut of the organization equivalent to the quantity of offers held as an extent of the organization's absolute exceptional offers.

• A trade posting means prepared liquidity for offers held by the organization's investors.

• It empowers the organization to raise extra assets by issuing more offers.

• Having traded on an open market offers makes it simpler to set up investment opportunities designs that are important to pull in capable representatives.

• Recorded organizations have more prominent perceivability in the commercial center; expert inclusion and request from institutional financial specialists can drive up the offer cost.

• Recorded offers can be utilized as money by the organization to make acquisitions in which part or the majority of the thought is paid in stock.

These advantages imply that most enormous organizations are open instead of private; exceptionally huge privately owned businesses, for example, sustenance and horticulture mammoth Cargill, mechanical combination Koch Industries, and DIY furniture retailer Ikea are the exemption as opposed to the standard.

Issues of Stock Exchange Listing

Yet, there are a few downsides to being recorded on a stock trade, for example,

• Critical expenses related with posting on a trade, for example, posting charges and greater expenses related with consistence and detailing.

• Oppressive guidelines, which may contract an organization's capacity to work together.

• The momentary focal point of most speculators, which powers organizations to attempt to beat their quarterly profit assesses as opposed to adopting a long haul strategy to their corporate methodology.

While this deferred posting may mostly be inferable from the downsides recorded over, the primary reason could be that well-overseen new companies with a convincing business recommendation approach remarkable measures of capital from sovereign riches reserves, private value, and financial speculators. Such access to apparently boundless measures of capital would make an IPO and trade posting significantly less of a problem that needs to be addressed for a startup.

Chapter 2:

Investment and Trading opportunities

The debate as to what constitutes speculation and what investment is one which has always raged in the financial community. Benjamin Graham in his book, The Intelligent Investor, was one of the first to put pen to paper and offer a definition. Subsequently, his many disciples such as Warren Buffett, Charlie Munger, etc. have built on that and have offered their own takes on it.

It is essential for you to understand the difference because the philosophy you most identify with will determine not only your approach to the markets but also whether you'll be successful or not. No one would expect a hardcore capitalist to support socialism and similarly, one can hardly be a successful speculator if investing is what appeals to you the most. Without going into too many technicalities, if you purchase anything with a view of treating it as an asset, you're investing. If you purchase something with the sole intention of selling it at a higher price without any care as to the underlying asset or what it represents, you're speculating.

As an example: Let's say someone offers you a book on personal financial advice for $100. You skim through this book and know that the information contained in it is priceless and that you'll probably save thousands and make a few more thousands by following its advice. Suddenly, $100 doesn't seem too steep a price for a book does it? You're investing your money in the book, and yourself, with the hope of using the book's advice to make even more money. You may or may not be able to implement this advice successfully but that's a risk you're willing to take.

Now let's say, when you're offered this book for $100, instead of skimming through this book to see what's in it, you first ask around to see what someone else is willing to pay for it. Let's assume someone you know says they'll pay $150 for it. You promptly buy the book for $100 and resell it for $150 for a quick profit. In this case, you're speculating that someone else is willing to pay a higher price for the book and you aren't particularly concerned with what the book is about. As long as there's someone willing to pay a higher price, you'll always buy that book.

It should come as no surprise to you that all forms of trading, day, swing, position, etc. firmly fall under the category of speculation. The example above simplifies the process a lot but you should understand the philosophy and approach behind speculation and check to see whether your beliefs are compatible or not. Most beginners only look at the money and forget this fundamental step in their education.

This is not to say that one approach is better than the other. You will find a lot of opinion columns on this subject but you will discover, as you progress in your learning, that investment vs speculation is a nonsensical debate. All that matters is you identify which one makes more sense and align yourself and your strategies accordingly.

Jim Douglas

Chapter 3:

Different Investment Opportunities

a. Stocks

While the stock market has long term trends that investors rely on fairly well as the years and decades go by, over the short term the stock market is highly volatile. By that, we mean that prices are fluctuating up and down and doing so over short time periods. Volatility is something that long-term investors ignore. It's why you will hear people that promote conservative investment strategies suggesting that buyers use dollar cost averaging. What this does is it averages out the volatility in the market. That way you don't risk making the mistake of buying stocks when the price is a bit higher than it should be, because you'll average that out by buying shares when it's a bit lower than it should be.

In a sense, over the short term, the stock market can be considered as a chaotic system. So from one day to the next, unless there is something specific on offer, like Apple introducing a new gadget that investors are going to think will be a major hit, you can't be sure what the stock price is going to be tomorrow or the day after that. An increase on one day doesn't mean more increases are coming; it might be followed by a major dip the following day. For example, at the time of writing, checking Apple's stock price, on the previous Friday it bottomed out at $196. Over the following days, it went up and down several times, and on the most recent close, it was $203. The movements over a short-term period appear random, and to a certain extent, they are. It's only over the long term that we see the actual direction that Apple is heading.

Of course, Apple is at the end of a ten-year run that began with the introduction of the iPhone and iPad. It's a reasonable bet that while it's a solid long-term investment, the stock probably isn't going to be moving enough for the purposes of making good profits over the short term from trades on call options (not too mention the per share price is relatively high).

The truth is volatility is actually a friend of the trader who buys call options. But it's a friend you have to be wary of because you can benefit from volatility while also getting in big trouble from it. The reason stocks with more volatility are the friend of the options trader is that in part the options trader is playing a probability game. In other words, you're looking for stocks that have a chance of beating the strike price you need in order to make profits. A volatile stock that has large movements has a greater probability of not only passing your strike price but doing so in such a fashion that it far exceeds your strike price enabling you to make a large profit.

Of course, the alternative problem exists – that the stock price will suddenly drop. That is why care needs to be a part of your trader's toolkit. A stock with a high level of volatility is just as likely to suddenly drop in price as it is to skip right past your strike price.

Moreover, while you're a beginner and might get caught with your pants down, volatile stocks are going to attract experienced options traders. That means that the stock will be in high demand when it comes to options contracts. What happens when there is a high demand for something? The price shoots up. In the case of call options, that means the stock will come with a higher premium. You will need to take the higher premium into account when being able to exercise your options at the right time and make sure the price is high enough above your strike price that you don't end up losing money.

Traders take some time to examine the volatility of a given stock over the recent past, but they also look into what's known as implied volatility. This is a kind of weather forecast for stocks. It's an estimate of the future price movements of a stock, and it has a large influence on the pricing of options. Implied volatility is denoted by the Greek symbol σ, implied volatility increases in bear markets, and it actually decreases when investors are bullish. Implied volatility is a tool that can provide insight into the options future value. For options traders, more volatility is a good thing. A stock that doesn't have much volatility is going to be a stable stock whose price isn't going to change very much over the lifetime of a contract. So while you may want to sell a covered call for a stock with low volatility, you're probably not going to want to buy one if you're buying call options because that means there will be a lower probability that the stock will change enough to exceed the strike price so you can earn a profit on a trade. Remember too that stocks that are very volatile will attract a lot of interest from options traders and command higher premiums. You will have to do some balancing in picking stocks that are of interest.

Being able to pick stocks that will have the right amount of volatility so that you can be sure of getting one that will earn profits on short term trades is something you're only going to get from experience. You should spend some time practicing before actually investing large amounts of money. That is, pick stocks you are interested in and make your bets but don't actually make the trades. Then follow them over the time period of the contract and see what happens. In the meantime, you can purchase safer call options, and so using this two-pronged approach gain experience that will lead to more surefire success down the road. One thing that volatility means for everyone is that predicting the future is an impossible exercise. You're going to have some misses no matter how much knowledge and experience you gain. The only thing to aim for is to beat the market more often than you lose. The biggest mistake you can make is putting your life savings into a single stock that you think is a sure thing and then losing it all.

b. Bonds

Bonds are commonly referred to fixed income securities, bonds are one among the three asset classes that individual investors are commonly familiar with, beside with stocks and also cash equivalents. A lot of government and corporate bonds are traded publicly; we have others that are traded just (OTC) that is over-the-counter or in privately between the lender and the borrower. When companies or even other entities require to bring up money to finance lucrative new projects, and maintain ongoing operations, they can also refinance existing debts, giving bonds straight to investors is also an option. The (issuer) gives a bond that do include the terms and rapport of the loan, the interest payments that are to be made, and also the time the loan (bond principal) is to be financed back, funds must and should be paid back (maturity date) as stipulated. The interest to be paid back (the coupon) is actually part of the return that the bondholders get earn for loaning their assets or funds to the issuer. Coupon rate is the term used to determine the interest rate.

c. Mutual funds

You can trade ETFs on the market through your brokerage account similar to how you would trade a regular company's stock such as Microsoft Corporation

(MSFT) or Apple Inc. (AAPL). You can buy them and sell them as a day trade or hold them longer for a swing trade. In the United States, most ETFs are set up as "open-ended" investment companies. This type of investment structure allows the funds to have greater flexibility in utilizing futures and options as well as being able to participate in security lending programs.

ETFs have been available to trade in the US for about 25 years now. In 2008, the US Securities and Exchange Commission proposed changes that essentially loosened the rules on the requirements for ETFs. Since then, these funds have grown dramatically in numbers and according to the "2017 Investment Company Fact Book", ETFs now make up about $2.5 trillion dollars in value.

These funds have changed significantly since the first broad-based index fund appeared in 1993. This first fund was set up to track the S&P 500 Index. You can think of an ETF as a pool of investments that the owners each own a piece of. The manager of the ETF will have a set of objectives and policies that will dictate the focus of the fund.

Today you can find ETFs that track virtually everything from indexes and bonds to stock sectors, commodities, currencies, and even the volatility of the market. Most recently, several firms have tried to create an ETF based on holding a basket of cryptocurrencies. ETFs can also be used to play both the long and short side of the market. If you suspect a sector like gold mining companies is dropping in price, then you can in effect go short on gold mining stocks by going long on DUST – an ETF that goes up in price when the prices of stock in gold mining companies drop.

To make things a little more interesting, some ETF managers have also created what is referred to as "beta" funds. These funds use derivatives like "options" and "futures" to magnify the movements of the underlying asset in the fund. For example, UNG is an ETF that moves with the price of natural gas, which can be quite volatile on its own. If that is not enough excitement for you, try UGAZ, which is another ETF that moves in sync with the price of natural gas except, through the use of these derivatives, it will move 3x in whatever direction the underlying natural gas asset does.

For example, let's say the price of natural gas jumps up 3% on an inventory report. If you hold the ETF UNG, the price will be up about the same 3%, but if you owned UGAZ, the price of that ETF would be up 9% (3 beta times 3%). You can easily see that owning UGAZ is great as long as the price of natural gas is going up, but it is very painful for an ETF holder if the price of natural gas drops, as the loss is correspondingly magnified.

Another issue with beta (also called leveraged) ETFs is that they need to be rebalanced at the end of each trading day. I will not go into the details on how the rebalancing process works, however, for those who are interested, please feel free to research this topic for yourself. There's quite a bit of information readily available online. It is important for the leveraged ETF investor to know that their leveraged holding can lose value over time, and especially in a volatile non-trending market. That means leveraged ETFs are better to hold in a trending market (either up or down) and should not be held for an extended period of time like a non-leveraged ETF or mutual fund.

The following are some of the reasons why an ETF can make for a good swing trade instrument.

• Expense ratios: ETFs have a relatively low expense ratio compared to other investment vehicles such as mutual funds. You always have to "pay to play" though, so try to keep these costs as low as possible.

• Ride a sector: let us imagine you really like the biotechnology space in general. There have been some mergers and acquisitions recently in this area and all of the stocks in the sector are reacting positively. Rather than going out and trying to buy up a basket of stocks in the sector, you can purchase an ETF like XBI, which invests in S&P stocks in the biotechnology sector. This is a much more cost-effective way to invest in a number of stocks in a sector without actually purchasing small numbers of numerous stocks.

• Risk management: using the same example of the biotechnology sector being hot, let's assume you decided to go out and buy a few individual stocks in this space instead of an ETF such as XBI. One of them could have been PUMA Biotechnology Inc. (PBYI). While XBI has been climbing higher through mid-January 2018, on January 23rd. PBYI finds out they will not be getting a key drug approval from Europe and the stock falls from $94.00 at the close to $65.00 after hours. In comparison, XBI experiences a small drop of about $2.00 per share on that same day. The bad news hurts XBI a bit but this small loss is nothing in comparison to what happened to those owning PBYI stock. Which would you rather own in this situation? This is a very fundamental principle of security ownership and highlights how bad it can be if you're not diversified in your portfolio.

d. Options

Options are a type of derivative that has an underlying financial asset, such as shares of stock. Most option traders are trading stock options. The option gives the buyer the right to buy or sell shares of stock at a fixed price, which is called the strike price. Options that give the buyer (of the option) the right to buy shares of stock are known as calls. If the option gives the buyer the right to sell shares of stock at the strike price, it's known as a put.

Option trading is amenable to swing trading because options are time-limited. Every options contract comes with an expiration date. The lifetime of an option can be quite varied, lasting from one week (so-called weekly) to a month, to several weeks, and even one year or more. Options that last one year or more are called LEAPs. However, no matter how long an option lasts, they all operate in basically the same fashion.

Unlike stocks, part of the pricing of an option is determined by "time value". The closer an option gets to the expiration date, the less time value the option has. That adds an extra wrinkle to trading options that other financial securities don't have – for example you can hold stocks for however long as you like. For details on how this operates, please download my book on Options Trading.

Since options (generally speaking) have a lifetime that fits well within the time periods that swing traders use, they naturally fit within a swing trading paradigm. A swing trader of options can use the same techniques of analysis that a swing trader of stocks or other financial assets will use to determine price swings. Puts offer an opportunity to short the market, so swing traders interested in shorting can use puts for that purpose rather than having to deal with the complexities and risks of using margin to borrow shares of stock.

Options have many strategies that specialists in options trading use to generate income, but those are not of interest to the swing trader. A swing trader will only be interested in using swings in stock price to profit from trading calls or puts at the right moment in time. This is a simpler approach rather than having to learn all the complicated schemes that have been put together to minimize risk with options. Instead, you will use the same tools to look for signals in the market that a swing trader of stocks is using, and then take advantage of buy and sell signals to buy or sell the appropriate options. The main difference will be focusing on the time value of the options and noting how that can impact pricing.

Jim Douglas

Chapter 4:

Details about Options

a. Call and Put Options

The second class of options is called a put option. Like any option, it has a strike price with an expiration date. But in this case, the buyer has the option to sell 100 shares of the underlying stock. The transaction would take place at the pre-arranged strike price before or during the expiration date of the option. These are called "puts," and this stems from the fact that the originator of the contract is forced to buy shares of stock, so the shares are "put to" the party who wrote the contract. Put options can be used in different ways. One way to profit from put options is by essentially shorting the stock. So when you buy a put option, you are short, believing that the stock will decline in price. Put options allow the owner to sell shares above the ongoing price on the market. That means they increase in value when the stock market declines.

Imagine that you buy a put options contract at $2 a share, for a stock trading at $50 a share. We could set the strike price to $48.

If the share price dropped to $46 a share or lower, you could buy the shares on the open market and then sell them to the originator of the put option at $48 a share.

Many options traders never exercise options but instead rely on being able to sell them at a profit to other traders before they expire. In the case of a put, you are still essentially shorting the stock because the price of the option will rise as stock price drops. In this case, you wouldn't buy the shares to sell to the writer of the put option, and you'd simply sell the put on the options market at a price that was higher than what you paid for it.

b. Options Trading Pros and Cons

Swing trading options are things that give the carrier the right, yet not the commitment, to either purchase or sell a measure of some basic resource at a pre-decided cost at or before the agreement lapses. Options can be obtained like most other resource classes with financier venture accounts.

Options are amazing in light of the fact that they can upgrade a person's portfolio. They do this through included pay, assurance, and even influence. Contingent upon the circumstance, there is normally an alternative situation fitting for a financial specialist's objective. A prominent model would utilize choices as a successful fence against a declining securities exchange to restrict drawback misfortunes. Alternatives can likewise be utilized to create repeating pay. Moreover, they are regularly utilized for theoretical purposes, for example, betting on the bearing of a stock.

There is nothing free with stocks and bonds and options are the same. They include certain dangers that the financial specialist must know about before making an exchange.

c. Pros of trading options

• Less time consuming than day trading. A trader is given more time in between trades to perform his/her analysis and could possibly choose better performers.

• An initial poor entry has time to recover and return to a positive state dependent upon the direction the trader has chosen. Long (up) positions will often fair better in this respect than an initial Short (down) position.

• Swing Traders need not be concerned with meeting the 'Pattern Day Trader' requirements.

• Swing traders are given more data to analyze (time frame wise) than are day traders. A swing trader has more confidence in his/her trade because the current trend is supported by longer term historical data.

d. Cons of trading options

Con: A Swing Trader can also get bad information into the mix of their data analysis and choose a less profitable performing stock or a losing stock.

• An initial poor entry has time to recover and return to a positive state dependent upon the direction the trader has chosen. Long (up) positions will often fair better in this respect than an initial Short (down) position.

Con: An initial poor entry also has time to keep moving against your trade.

A swing trader, day trader or any 'trader' must be aware at all times of what they are doing and what they could expect from any given trade. Here is a brief check list of very basic things to analyze before entering into a trade along with a little tip.

Jim Douglas

78

Chapter 5:
Risk Management Strategies

Risk management is a grossly neglected area of every unsuccessful trader's strategy. Indeed, most do not even understand the concept and fail to explore it beyond the cursory nod given to stop losses and per trade risk.

Here's the thing: Perfect risk management can save a poor strategy but even the best strategy cannot save poor risk management. Many of you must have heard of this piece of wisdom but probably very few of you truly understand its implications.

You see, most people enter the world of trading with dreams of dollar signs and massive money in a short period of time. They aren't concerned with the possibility of loss and only consider the massive gains on offer. Such traders (gamblers is a more apt term) soon find themselves in the red and either quit in disgust or even worse, attack the markets with new capital and a shiny, new, "infallible" strategy.

a. Diversification

The second major strategy that buy and hold investors use is diversification. They want to invest in a large number of stocks so that while individual stocks might have ups and downs, the overall portfolio tracks the market. They are satisfied matching market returns. In fact, many buy and hold investors take this to the extreme, investing only in index funds that track major indices such as the S & P 500. These types of investors don't even do much fundamental analysis, and it's a strategy that requires little day-to-day attention.

As you can see, there are many differences between long-term investors and swing traders. While the long-term investor is attempting to build up a diversified portfolio over years and decades, a swing trader may be focused on one or two stocks, and exit the positions in a matter of days. While buy and hold investors are satisfied tracking overall market performance, swing traders seek to beat overall market performance. Swing traders utilize the tools of technical analysis in order to find the right entry and exit points of their trades. Long-term investors ignore them and don't care about short term fluctuations or swings.

b. Basic Money Management

- Money Management Strategy 1: Martingale

You can ask any gambler around and, believe me, they know what this strategy is about like they would know their ABC's. The idea is straight forward and simple: as you lose more, you increase your risk. For example, if you risk $50 and lose, you need to bet $100 on the next turn. If that doesn't quite work, bet $200. After a long enough losing streak, theoretically and statistically, you will win. And, if you have doubled your risk right from the onset, that single win could recoup your initial loses and, if you are fortunate enough, even gain some profit.

The question, however, is this: do you have enough to finally win and make it back? Unless you have an unlimited amount of money to spend, this is hardly a reliable strategy. There are a lot of newbie Forex traders who adopt this strategy. Unsurprisingly, it leads not only to great losses but, much worse, to wipe-outs!

- Money Management Strategy 2: Anti-Martingale

The anti-Martingale is the opposite of the above money management strategy. The idea is to increase your risk when you are winning and tone it down when you are losing. Like the Martingale strategy, this is high-risk, but it's perfect for traders who want higher returns while still keeping their initial balance. There are many experienced Forex traders who adopt this money management strategies, and with good results!

- Money Management Strategy 3: One Percent Risk Rule

This system has saved many traders from total bankruptcy and wipeouts. The beauty in this strategy is that it's simple and effective. The name says it all: for every trade, you should adjust your risk to roughly 1 percent of your account's balance. Here's an example: let's say your account has $1,000,000. One percent of it is equal to $10,000. That means your Stop Loss should be tweaked so that, for every trade you go into, you will not lose more than $10,000. Simple and effective, indeed, but why is it that only a handful of traders adopt this? The answer is that they are not looking for moderate profits. They want to hit it big in as little time as possible.

c. Hedging with Options

The easiest way to understand hedging is to think of it as insurance. When you hedge, you are insuring yourself against a negative event. This does not mean that once you hedge the negative event will not happen, but instead if it does happen the impact of the event is reduced. An example is like getting a car insurance.

With Forex hedging, you are essentially placing a bet in both directions of the market. You are placing a buy and a sell order on the currency pairs. This allows you to hedge your bet to reduce your risk in the Forex market and potentially profit from movement in either direction. This requires training and if done properly, it is a good skill to have as a Forex trader.

In Forex hedging, there are essentially a few types of hedging strategies

• Buy and sell the same currency pair, same lot in the almost the same timing. After some time, one order will gain while the other will lose. When the winner run out of steam, take profit and wait for the losing trade to turn around. This strategy work well in a yo-yo kind of market trend.

Example: buy 1 lot EUR/USD at 1.3400 and sell 1 lot EUR/USD at 1.3397. If the price goes up to 1.3460 and we close the order to take 60 pips while the sell order has a drawdown of 63 pips. In such market condition, the rate will start to fall. If the rate fall to 1.3420 and you close the sell order with a loss of 23 pips. Overall, we have gain 60 pips - 23 pips = 37 pips. Experience trader typically use technical analysis skills to decide their entry and exit points.

However, such strategy is no longer allowed if you have the right broker that adheres to National Futures Association (NFA) rules. If you sign up with a FOREX broker that is not in the NFA, you can still employ such hedging strategy in your account. For those that still wish to use hedging, there are a number of ways to do so.

• Hedging using correlated pairs

Use currency pairs that have a good and strong correlation. On the other hand, there are some currencies that reflect each other as they gradually move. The move can be directly or inversely proportional to each other. Let's look at on example, Let us say you take look at the charts of USD /EUR and also CHF/ USD pairs, you'll find that there are very close parallel trend looking at the patterns on the graphs. This means that traders can use the similarity in intent to try and reduce the losses and position yourself to build a hedging formula that could effectively combine these two currency which pairs. Since USD/CHF and EUR/USD move and change inversely one can potentially BUY the both pairs. Result will reflect that one order will comfortably gain profit, and another will lose. Thus they will have cancel each other out. Hence, one can formulate a profitable avenue hedge strategy comparable to item 1.

• There are also other forms of hedging being employed, such as Hedging arbitrage - This technique involves getting 2 brokers. One charge interest and one do not. Buy from the broker that the currency pair that provides you rollover interest and sell from the broker that does not charge rollover interest. This way, you can gain the interest or SWAP that is credited to your account. Be careful not to get margin call, so managing the two accounts by transferring money from one account to another is crucial so that you have enough funds in.

d. Changing your Mindset

Having the right mindset means everything when you want to succeed as a swing trader. You must employ specific techniques that will enable you to put the emotion out of your trading so that you can make pragmatic decisions that result in profitability for you.

There are a number of ways of investing intelligently so that you can succeed whenever you start trading different types of financial instruments. You must have a specific marketing and trading psychology in order for you to succeed in your endeavors. Trading success comes when an individual has the correct devices to investigate and understand the market just as the best possible mentality that enables them to remain in the stream and not think excessively or break down something over the top.

Thinking in excess of is genuinely a type of mental toxic substance that whenever left unchecked, can devour you and definitely change your reasoning, conduct and even your character. Obviously, this pessimistic propensity can have heartbreaking outcomes in any everyday issue: work, individual connections, school and particularly in exchanging.

Likewise, with most things, a gifted broker is at his or her best when they are at the time and not pondering all the potential results of a specific exchange. Exchanging is certifiably not a round of chess like such a significant number of individuals assume. It will not improve your chances of achievement by deduction more, investigating more or being at your graphs more, on the off chance that it was that simple everybody would do it. Overthinking can appear as though an expansive and to some degree darken point so it is critical to characterize what it is so you know when or in the event that you are doing it so you can begin making a move to stop it.

We as a whole realize that on the off chance that somebody is over thinking, they are considering a subject, to the point where it contrarily impacts them.

One sure-fire approach to get your synapses out of an overthinking limbo is to begin seeing brief time period outlines. The principle purpose behind underscoring exchanging the higher time allotment graphs is on the grounds that it rearranges your investigation and smoothens out all the clamor and arbitrary value activity on the brief span outlines. This clamor and haphazardness make you over think and overtrade and by and large just disrupts your exchanging. On the off chance that you have been tailing news for any huge period of time, you realize that for the most part, people loathe exchanging the news since they feel the value activity mirrors every appropriate variable of a market and furthermore in light of the fact that it makes dealers over think and over-exchange.

There are a huge number of factors that can influence a market at some random minute, so honestly, to attempt to examine or exchange the news is fundamentally a similar thing as attempting to out-think the market or imagining that in the event that you simply realize more you will make sense of the following move. All that is genuine is that the value activity is as of now demonstrating to you what the effect of any news on a market, so skirt all the additional news and simply figure out how to peruse the impression of the market; the value activity.

As a retail swing trader or a retail dealer of any market, there are numerous powers neutralizing you, which you may or not have known about as of not long ago. To be completely forthright with you, you are a one-person group when you are a merchant, and except if you approach incredibly enormous entireties of cash or the capacity to withstand huge problems, you are not going to keep going extremely long on the off chance that you do not utilize the best possible trading strategy.

In the event that exchanging appears to be baffling and hard to you, do not stress, you are not the only one. Numerous brokers, if not most, start their exchanging professions with grandiose objectives and a full tank of expectation; however those things can blur in all respects rapidly on the off chance that you aren't moving toward the market from the right 'point'.

The huge players in the market, similar to banks, speculative stock investments, and so forth know where littler retail merchants put in their requests and what they regularly do in the market, purchase breakouts, day-exchange, and so forth. They know all the little clock procedures and, in all honesty, they appreciate taking your cash each day in the market. You cannot get by without a stop misfortune, however they can, or possibly they can for any longer than you might predict and this is the reason day exchanging is perilous; in light of the fact that dealers put extremely little or tight stop misfortunes on their positions they frequently get halted out by typical day by day value vacillations in the market.

It is not right to state that your agent needs you to lose, yet saying they need you to day-exchange is a reasonable evaluation. For what reason do they need you to day-exchange you inquire? Indeed, for one you will produce a great deal of charges as spread installments or commissions, and two, you will lose a ton of exchanges. So, day-exchanging is a trick's down that sucks individuals in by speaking to their voracious and anxious want to make quick cash.

On the furthest edge of the exchanging scale, we have position exchanging or contributing, this is fundamentally long haul purchase and hold systems that while they may satisfy when you are prepared to resign, they are not appropriate for anybody hoping to bring home the bacon as a broker, similar to what you think. That carries us to what is called the exchanging sweet spot; swing exchanging. On the off chance that you do not definitely know, this is what swing exchanging is: Swing Trading is a strategy for specialized examination to enable you to spot solid directional moves in the market that keep going all things considered, two to six days. Swing trading permits singular merchants like us to misuse the solid transient moves made by huge institutional brokers who can't move all through the market as fast.

It is also necessary to understand what a swing point is in the market in order to have the right psychology to trade. To place this in a little more straightforward terms, it is necessary to accept you have taken a gander at a fundamental value outline previously. On the off chance that you have, you likely seen that business sectors do not move in straight lines for long. Rather, cost will swing from high to depressed spots in the market. Particularly in an inclining market, these diagram swing focuses are basic focuses on a value outline where we can envision a value activity sign to frame at, and that frequently give high-likelihood passages just before a pattern is preparing to continue. Swing exchanging is the workmanship and ability of perusing a value diagram to envision the following swing in the market. It is necessary to use value activity exchanging systems to discover high-likelihood passages in the market at these swing focuses. You may see me allude to this as purchasing shortcomings or purchasing the plunges in a rising business sector and selling quality. This phrasing alludes to the general methodology that a swing merchant utilizes; purchasing as a market tumbles down and ideally purchasing the swing depressed spot or near it inside an up-slanting business sector, the inverse would be the situation for a down pattern obviously.

There are different reasons why you ought to turn into a swing dealer if you can handle the psychology of trading; since swing exchanging has been discussed in detail, is and the primary motivation behind why you have to learn it and make it your exchanging strategy, how about we examine a portion of different advantages of it.

As explained, when you exchange the day by day diagram time span as a swing dealer does, you are receiving numerous rewards contrasted with those poor spirits who still think scalping a five-minute graph is the way to progress.

One reason why swing exchanging is such a tremendous favorable position to the retail merchant, is that it enables you to skirt all the market clamor of brief time periods, similar to those under the one-hour outline. Representatives and the enormous institutional dealers want littler retail brokers to exchange brief time allotments and day-exchange/scalp, since they realize they will get your cash effectively in the event that you do.

Swing exchanging on higher time spans like the four hour and every day enables you to piggyback off the enormous moves made by the greater players in the market, and it likewise enables you to put your stop misfortune outside of their achieve, in this way giving you more noteworthy fortitude with the goal that you can remain in the market longer and increment your odds of getting on board a major, gainful move. Swing trading enables you to fit exchanging around whatever bustling timetable you may have, or in the event that you don't have a bustling calendar it will enable you to make cash exchanging and still make the most of your spare time. There is nothing more exhausting than sitting before the outlines throughout the day, also that it is terrible for your exchanging and your wellbeing.

Swing trading enables you to break down the business sectors on your calendar, for brief timeframes, in light of the fact that you are concentrating on higher time allotments as referenced previously. Likewise, on the grounds that you are holding your exchanges for multi-day or more much of the time, you can enter an exchange on a Tuesday suppose, at that point rest and get up multi day later and keep an eye on your exchange. You do not have to stay there throughout the night agonizing over your exchanges, nor should you. A nearly mysterious thing happens when you quit giving such a great amount of consideration to your exchanges; you begin to see better-exchanging outcomes.

Individuals over-muddle their exchanging by just being excessively included. Swing exchanging is the best technique since it is integral to how you ought to carry on in the market since it rewards you for being less included and taking fewer exchanges after some time, which is actually what you have to on the off chance that you like to get any opportunity at progress. The bring-home message here is, swing exchanging will enable you to stay away from over-exchanging, and over-exchanging is the most compelling motivation why individuals lose their cash exchanging.

Try not to be tricked by the showcasing and contrivance exchanging frameworks out there. On the off chance that you have been around the exchanging hinder a couple of times as of now you most likely hear what is being discussed here. There are a ton of guarantees and assurances out there in the exchanging scene, yet the inquiry you ought to posture is not about certifications yet about the strategy itself. Is the technique really going to train me to comprehend a value diagram and how to get enormous moves in the market? Is it really going to show me how to exchange appropriately? These are simply the kinds of inquiries you should pose to yourself about any exchanging framework or training you are thinking about, in light of the fact that these are ones that issue. Try not to fall prey to enormous cases of quick cash and completely computerized exchanging robots; recollect, on the off chance that it sounds unrealistic, it most likely is.

e. Controlling Addictions

Your most important objective in any type of trading is to manage your risk. The objective is not to buy and sell stocks – it is to make a profit. Your broker is the only winner when you are buying and selling stocks in the market. Your job is to manage your risk and your account. Whenever you click "buy" or "sell" (going short) on your trading platform, you expose your money to a risk of loss.

An unsuccessful trader will likely look at an entry and only think about how much they are going to make on a trade. A successful trader will always consider what is the upside and what is the downside on any particular trade. In other words, how much am I risking if I have to take a loss? This is not about being right on a trade or being wrong; it is about comparing the risk you are taking to the reward you hope to get from the trade. If you are risking a loss of $0.50 per share on a trade and only expect to get $0.25 per share as the upside reward, then this is NOT a good risk to reward ratio.

To have a good trade setup, you should expect to get at least 2 times the reward in comparison to the risk that you are taking. Obviously, having more than 2 times the reward is even better. If you use this risk to reward strategy in your trading, you will still be marginally profitable even if you are wrong 60% of the time.

Let's look at a setup for a good swing trade and how we can assess the risk compared to the reward. On February 11th a trader is looking at the chart of the ETF XBI and notices a nice setup for buying some shares (going long). The basic principles of why this trade setup looks good for a long will be discussed in the following chapters. Referring to Figure 5.1 below, an experienced swing trader would look at this chart and determine that if they went long on XBI at $87.50 per share, they would risk $1.00 per share ($87.50-$86.50=$1.00). At around the $86.50 level (the low close of a recent price move), a swing trader would consider the trade a failure and they would sell the position for a loss.

For the reward, they are hoping XBI gets to $91.00 per share (a prior area of resistance which I will discuss later in the book) for a possible gain of $3.50 per share ($91.00-$87.50=$3.50). In this setup, the trader is risking $1.00 per share to make $3.50 per share. That is a very good risk to reward ratio, and in this particular example you can see it worked exactly as expected, with XBI easily hitting the target price of $91.00.

Chapter 6:
Swing Trading with Call Options

a. How to Swing Trade

Swing exchanging depends on distinguishing swings in stocks, items, and monetary standards that occur over a time of days. A swing exchange may take a couple of days to half a month to work out. In contrast to an informal investor, a swing merchant isn't probably going to make exchanging a full-time profession.

Anybody with information and venture capital can have a go at swing exchanging. On account of the more extended time period, from days to weeks instead of minutes to hours, a swing broker shouldn't be stuck to his PC screen throughout the day. He can even keep up a different all-day work as long as he isn't checking exchanging screens all the time at work.

Exchanges for the most part need time to work out. Keeping an exchange for a benefit open for a couple of days or weeks may result in higher benefits than exchanging and out of a similar security on various occasions multi day. Swing exchanging should be possible with only one PC and customary exchanging apparatuses. It does not require the best in class innovation of day trading.

The swing broker can set stop misfortunes. While there is a danger of a quit being executed at a horrible value, it beats the consistent checking of every vacant position that are a component of day exchanging.

Likewise, with any style of exchanging, swing exchanging can likewise result in considerable misfortunes. Since swing dealers hold their situations for longer than informal investors, they additionally risk bigger misfortunes.

Since swing exchanging more often than not includes positions held at any rate medium-term, edge necessities are higher. Most extreme influence is normally multiple times one's capital. Contrast this and day exchanging where edges are multiple times one's capital.

Since swing exchanging is only here and there an all-day work, there is considerably less possibility of burnout because of stress. Swing brokers normally have a customary activity or another wellspring of salary from which they can counterbalance or relieve exchanging misfortunes.

b. How to find the support and resistance

You will often start with a scan of the market to identify possible trade opportunities. Once some potential trades are identified, you should look at the charts to see if you can identify levels of support and resistance.

Let's imagine you have a particular stock that during a scan has been identified as a potential long trade. This is a price where it has not been able to break higher in the past. You would probably want to pass on going long on this stock because this is an area of prior price resistance.

Alternatively, if you find a stock that is trading just above a level of prior support, this may provide a good long entry from a risk to reward perspective. Your risk would be the price difference from the support level to the entry price. Next, you would look to find where you might expect the stock price to meet some resistance and then calculate your risk to reward ratio. Recall that your potential reward should be at least 2 times the risk you are taking on the trade.

The stock price fluctuates between these 2 levels giving opportunities to go long and to go short as shown in the figure. At the break of support in August, you would have quickly been stopped out or not have taken that trade at all due to the gap down and erratic price action.

There is a pause at the previous level of support before news related to the stock results in a gap and go price movement. The news was particularly good because the upper prior level of resistance did not stop the stock from moving higher after a very short pause.

c. Where to place your stop-loss and why

A Stop Loss order is placed to protect the trader from losing more money on a trade than they are willing to risk. A trader opens a position either long or short a trading vehicle. At the same time the smart trader will enter a Stop Loss order opposite the opening trade. If the first order was a buy, the Stop Loss will be a sell order for the same number of units. This helps to keep emotion out of a trade or making it a hope trade. "I hope it quits losing me money soon" is a hope trade. Do Not Begin Trading without an order to protect your capital. Hope trades are for amateurs, and will cause only losses, be it in the stock market, the futures market or the Currency Market.

Although many traders do not use this method of trading, the traders that do use them are more likely to be winning traders in the long run. They have analyzed the trade and have a very good idea of how much risk they are willing to accept as part of the trade. If the trade goes against them, the Stop Loss will protect the capital and keep the loss at an acceptable level. Without an order in place, the trader has to manually get out of the position by putting in an order to close the position. This is where the good trader and the lucky trader part company. The good trader controls losses and the lucky trader just depends on being able to move when he is forced to move. This where the trade can turn into a hope trade and the trader lets emotion control the trade rather than logic. This is the easiest way to turn a small loss into a big loss. Do not be a fool and trade without Stop Loss orders.

Placing Stop Loss orders is an art form and there are considerations to be made. One is where to place it, perhaps at the level in which the trader first entered into the trade. Traders might prefer a trailing stop loss to protect a profitable trade. The trailing stop could be used as the trade makes money. Entering new orders and canceling the old order at the same time makes this a trailing stop. This can also be used as a way to further protect a profitable trade by closing up the current price level and the stop order price. Eventually the order will be triggered, but the profit may be greater than just getting out of the trade by feel. As with all trading, the idea is to use as little risk as possible and still give the trade some breathing room.

Stop Loss orders should be used at entry and then later to keep as much of the profit as possible. These are two very distinct and different uses of this valuable order. It means lower losses and more possible profit.

Remember that Forex Trading involves substantial risk as well as chance for substantial profit. Protect yourself with Stop Losses and other tools at your disposal, and trade wisely.

d. Picking the Right Trades: Swing Trading with Call Options

A call option is an agreement that gives the buyer the option to purchase stocks. The benefit to the buyer is the agreement contains a pre-arranged price, which is called the strike price.

Remember that all options contracts are optional for the buyer, which is the buyer of a call option is not obligated to purchase the shares. Buying a call option is a long investment, which is you are bullish on the stock and hope to profit from a rise in the share price. This can be done in one of two ways. The first way is to simply purchase the shares at their strike price if the market price of the shares has risen above the strike price. That way, the buyer benefits from being able to purchase the stock on a reduced price after the price of the shares has risen, possibly substantially. Then either they can turn around and sell them at a profit on the stock market or they could be satisfied that they were able to buy stocks at a lower price.

The second, and far more common way to profit would be to trade the option, that is, sell it to another buyer for a profit. An options trader can do this because when share prices rise in comparison to the strike price, demand for that option rises, driving up the price for the option. This is how most traders earn money trading options. So you could buy an option for $100, and then sell it for $150 a few days later.

Jim Douglas

Chapter 7:
Understanding Chart Patterns

a. Trading patterns

We continue our look at tools that can help traders win at more trades while swing trading by taking a closer look at chart patterns. Some chart patterns can contain a wealth of information that you can just eyeball from the chart rather than diving into deep and complicated analysis. In this chapter we will look at some of the most important chart patterns and explain how they can be used to determine when to enter and exit your trades.

ABCD Patterns

The ABCD pattern is another one of the basic and relatively easy patterns to recognize and trade. It is essentially a price move higher or lower, followed by a flag and then a continuation of a trend. As with much technical analysis-based trading, it often works because so many traders and computers are watching for the pattern and subsequently trading this setup. It becomes another one of those self-fulfilling prophecies I discussed previously in this book.

This pattern is based on the principle that stock prices move in waves. These waves are due to the fact that price control is continually moving between the buyers and the sellers. If you examine a daily price chart of any stock, you will see waves of fluctuation up and down. Then, if you compare that daily chart to a weekly chart of the same stock, you will also see waves, but they will likely have larger price ranges because you're looking at a longer period of time. Within each one of those weekly bars there are 5 1-day bars, creating smaller waves inside bigger waves.

Knowing that stocks are moving in waves allows you to play on those waves much like a surfer. As a swing trader, you are waiting to catch and ride a wave, but like surfing, timing is very important. You will never see a surfer starting to paddle like crazy at the top of a wave to catch a ride. They wait to begin their ride as the wave is just starting to approach. Similarly, a trader needs to anticipate the next wave and get on board at the beginning of the next move in price action

Bullish ABCD patterns start with a strong upward move. The buyers are aggressively buying a stock from point A and consistently making new highs of the day (point B). You should not enter the trade here because at point B the price action is very extended. More importantly, your stop-loss will be way below your entry, giving you an extremely poor risk to reward ratio. As I discussed earlier, you should be looking for at least 2 times the reward for the risk that you are taking. Using our surfer analogy, that wave snuck up on us and passed us by, so we wait for the next wave.

At point B, the traders who bought the stock earlier start selling it for profit and the price comes down. You should still not enter the trade because you do not know where the bottom of this pullback will be. However, if you see that the price does not come down from a certain level, such as point C, it means that the stock has found a potential support. You can now plan your trade in the same manner that I described previously for trading flags and pendants. You should decide on an entry price, a stop out level and an exit point(s) for a profit.

Bearish ABCD patterns are the reverse of the bullish pattern, with the stock price heading lower initially, and then there will be a bounce, which will be followed by a continuation lower.

Let's look at an example of an ABCD trade on Advanced Micro Devices, Inc. (AMD) in Figure 9.8. The price action on this stock creates a very tradable pattern for a short trade. AMD pulls back from a high at point A to level B. It then forms a nice bear flag and also creates a double top when it fails to break through the previous high. I have already discussed the double top and flag patterns. The alignment of these patterns are all telling you the same thing, making this an excellent setup for you to take a short position on AMD.

The stop-out price level on the short would be a break higher at about the $12.50 level. A failure of the stock to move higher would have allowed you to hold the position as it moved lower, possibly scaling out instead of selling the position for a profit all at once. By scaling out, you can lock in some profits and keep moving the stop out price lower as the price moves lower to maximize the gain on the trade.

An illustration of 2 ABCD patterns (bearish and bullish).

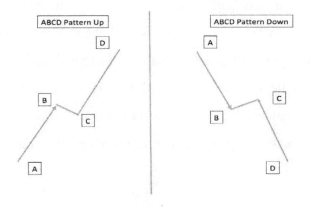

How to Trade ABCD Patterns

The real key to trading this pattern is to watch for the pullbacks that inevitably occur when a stock makes a push higher or lower. Look for those bull or bear flags to form and plan your entries, exits and stops accordingly, as I discussed earlier in the previous section.

These patterns will often end with a double bottom or double top pattern. This is another pattern I have discussed earlier and like to use as a trade setup. A topping pattern will usually have one or more gravestone type doji and the price action will struggle to make a new high and then ultimately fail and move lower. A bottoming pattern will be the reverse – one or more doji will make a dragonfly pattern signaling that the sellers are exhausted and the buyers are starting to take control. These signals do not necessarily have to appear but they help to confirm a setup for an entry on a trade.

To summarize my trading strategy for the ABCD pattern:

• You look for stocks in a strong uptrend or downtrend. You will find these by using a scan (discussed later in this book) or through some other source such as social media.

• You then watch for the stock to transition into a consolidation period where the price action becomes choppy for a period of time.

• As the choppy price action continues, you draw your lines of support and resistance and plan your trade with an entry point, stop-loss price and exit strategy for a profit.

• You enter the trade when the price hits your entry point and then you follow your trading plan, taking profits either by a single sale or by scaling out if you think the trend will continue. If the trade does not go as expected, you stop out, take the loss and move on to the next opportunity.

b. Head and Shoulders

A head and shoulders pattern is a peak, followed by a larger or higher peak, and then followed by another peak that is about the height of the first peak. The "head" forms the middle while the two smaller peaks flanking it are the "shoulders". In other words, the price keeps moving up but hitting a limit and then moving back down to a floor pricing level. In the middle peak, it goes to a higher price.

A head and shoulders pattern is considered a reliable indicator of a coming trend reversal. Typically, it may be seen after a long bullish trend, so it's a solid indicator that the bullish trend is over and a downturn in price is in the near future.

How to Trade Head and Shoulders Patterns

This pattern offers a number of different entry options. It is possible that you can pick it up as a double bottom if the second move was not that exaggerated. In other words, if the head part of the pattern was not too extended from the right shoulder. This entry gives you the best risk to reward because you are getting an entry near the lowest point of the pattern and the risk is clearly defined as the extreme price of the head.

The second possibility for an entry is at the left shoulder. This entry is not as attractive because your stop out level could still be at the extreme high or low of the head portion of the pattern. If the left shoulder is trading

119

sideways for an extended period, you can draw a line of support on the bottom or top of the pattern and use that as a stop out price level.

Many traders will use the break of the neckline to go short on a head and shoulders or to go long on the inverse of the pattern. Once the price breaks through the neckline, strong moves usually follow. This allows you to set your stop price around the neckline, which will exit you from the trade on a failed move. Figure 9.10 includes entry points for this trade as well as levels where you should stop out if the price action does not follow through as hoped.

How to Trade Flag Patterns

Flag patterns require a little patience while you wait for the flag to form after the initial run up or drop. Once you have recognized the beginning of the pattern, you should start to plot the upper and lower trendlines as they form. These trendlines will be one of your potential entry points and/or stop out levels.

You will usually have 2 possible entry spots on any flag formation in order to play the continuation of the trend. The first possible entry is on the break of the trendline. The second entry option occurs when the price action breaks the high or low of the flagpole (depending on whether it is an uptrend or downtrend continuation).

The first entry will get you into the position a little earlier, which will allow you to profit more on the next surge in price action (up or down). The downside of getting in earlier is that there is always the potential for the stock to have a failed breakout and not move in the direction you expect. Waiting a little longer for the break in the top of the flag results in a little higher probability of a successful trade.

These flag patterns also give you 2 stop-loss price level options to use in case the stock does not move in the direction expected. If the stock fails to follow through and continue the trend, then the trendlines can provide a price level for a stop. On a downtrend, you would use the upper resistance line in the flag and in an uptrend you would use the lower support line.

The second stop-loss option is to use the low of the lowest candle in the bull flag and the high of the highest candle in a bear flag. If you are a more conservative trader, you would use the closer stop price to keep losses to a minimum. However, this may result in getting stopped out of a trade that is becoming more volatile as the trend starts to continue. This means that, while you may take a smaller loss with this stop out price level, using this level may result in missing the move you were intending to play by getting stopped out due to some volatility in price. This volatility component is why some traders will give the trade a little more room to avoid having their stop triggered due to some volatility as opposed to a real direction change. Therefore, they will place their stop at the lower support trend line on uptrends and at the higher resistance trend line on downtrends.

A more sophisticated or experienced trader might use multiple entries and exits to offset some of the risks of entering the trade too early. A smaller percentage of the total trade in shares can be used as a starter position and then added to at the second point above or below the flagpole.

Figure below shows a chart of Caterpillar, Inc. (CAT) in a nice uptrend with 4 bull flags over a month-long period before the trend reverses. Notice the double top that takes place as I discussed in the previous section, giving a clear indication that the upward trend is out of energy and a reversal in price is about to happen. After the reversal, there are several bear flags formed on the overall trend down as bargain hunters think the bottom is forming and they go long. Traders who went short at the double top start taking profits, giving a temporary lift in the stock's price before the selling continues.

c. Cup and Handle

The cup and handle, in contrast to the spike reversals, reveals a strangely slow shift in the given trend. Mostly and often seen at bottoms, the cup and handle pattern do represent a slow and a more gradual change in the given trend from down and also sideways, then up, ultimately. The chart picture resembles a cup or handle—therefore the name is derived.

Looking at the chart you can always see little price movement during the formation of the Saucer. For almost a year the stock stays in the $10 trading range with very little variation in price. You will notice two peaks during this time period. It looks like it tried to muster up the energy to advance, but simply didn't have the momentum to do it. Owning a stock like this will put you to sleep. However, this is a perfect type setup to put on your stock alerts.

For instance: If you are perusing stock charts and see a stock in this formation. You might want to set an alert to notify you if the stock 'breaks out.'

In this particular case, an alert could have been set for $18 or $20 dollars. Just above the last known resistance. Then if the stock hit that price you would be alerted that a possible break out was happening. At that point you could wait for confirmation, check the volume on the breakout, and then buy. The confirmation would be a close above those peaks in the center of the rounded bottom. Therefore a close in the $20 range on good volume would confirm that the break out was in place.

The small peaks in the middle of this cup formation are really what most would consider false breakout attempts. Sure there are those who might have bought the stock at the bottom, around $5 per share, and got lucky when it advanced a few bucks and took a quick profit. But until a stock like this can trade above the last known resistance, it is just treading water. Another thing to consider is the stock's price. A $5 stock is normally not a strong stock that everyone wants to own. It is barely above the penny-stock value and most of these do not have the buying interest to make significant advances. In other words, when there are no buyers, there's no advance.

d. Triangles

Symmetrical Triangle

You will see this pattern during upward trends. It is like the stock has moved up from a lower price level, and just needs to 'take a breather,' so it pauses and consolidates.

While watching one of these patterns form, there are several things that cross the mind of a trader.

First of all, early on when the price moved up to around $50 the second time, but didn't reach the previous high, the first thing that would come to mind as a trader/investor would be "that is a double top." But the stock pulls back and holds above the previous low, so there is no reason to sell since the last known support (the previous low) held. In fact, it made a higher low which is good. The only problem at that point is the lower high it made. But then it advances again and makes another lower high. At this point, with two highs and two lows, a trend and channel line can be drawn creating the triangle. At that point most traders are going to wait to see if a break out occurs before buying, or a drop below the last support occurs before selling.

That explains why there is less buying on the advances, thus the lower highs. It just becomes a waiting game. They are not going to buy without a breakout and certainly not going to short sell a strong stock that is making higher lows. But see what happened as soon as the stock advanced to break out above the old previous high? Yes! It 'Gapped' up the next day.

The buying interest returned… Look at the volume on the breakout as well. The higher volume tells us that there were many traders and investors waiting for the breakout.

Do you see that the 'Gap' at the breakout was closed a few days later? It took a week or so, but the stock traded back down to where the gap occurred to close it. You can also see that there were several gaps on that chart, and most were closed. That is just something to keep in mind. More often than not, gaps are closed.

Ascending Triangle

The ascending triangle looks like a complete replica to the symmetrical triangle This looks similar to this Ascending Triangle, except the descending triangle has got a declining sort of an upper channel line and usually a near flat lower trend line. This would indicate that the sellers are also more aggressive than even the buyers. So this is a bearish pattern.

The descending triangle usually forces a trader to wait and see what will happen. But the formation itself suggests it is bearish. Although there are no lower lows being made, it is just holding support. In the mind of a trader, the lower highs indicate weakness, and each lower high suggests more weakness. So it always appears it is just a matter of time until the support fails to hold.

Realistically, the stock only has two options. It either has to eventually break out above the declining channel line or fall through support. And the lower highs tell us the selling pressure is becoming stronger. So it becomes a squeeze.

Talking about Trend Lines, Descending lines, Ascending lines, Flat Bottoms, Bullish and Neutral, etc, it may get rather confusing. But when you look at the formation of a Triangle Pattern, the "Descending Triangle" having the flat bottom would tell you that the Buyers are not that excited – if they were, the bottom would not be flat – It would be ascending. Therefore it is a weak pattern that may not have the strength or momentum to advance.

Yet the symmetrical and ascending triangles are showing strength with the higher lows. Therefore, they are more likely to be advancing.

Another way to look at, and interpret a triangle is this: When you look at the wide end of the left side of a triangle, and then follow the lines to the point (Apex), it becomes rather obvious that something has got to give. It's like squeezing a juice box from the bottom up. The more pressure that is applied, the more likely the juice is going to squirt out the straw.

That is why when the bottom trend line of the triangle is in an upward trend that is a pretty clear indication that the buyers are more aggressive. And eventually they are likely to win the battle and the price will move higher.

Yet, when the bottom is flat, the buyers are not as aggressive; they are just holding and waiting. There are possibly a few new buyers that are buying at the support, but even those buyers are waiting for the stock to reach the support before buying, thus, no higher lows.

In the chart, you can always notice when the stock finally brakes below the support, many of those who were holding and waiting suddenly became sellers. This caused a dramatic drop very quickly, not to mention other traders who jumped in to short-sell the stock. But you can see there are about three daily candles just under the support level. This tells us that there would have been time to exit the position once support was broken before the stock eventually fell by $10 per share or more.

The point is, the use of a stop loss would have prevented a huge loss by selling you out quickly. If your stop loss was just under the support level – you would have been sold out and avoided the loss.

e. Golden Cross

For the swing trader, golden cross is important to use for spotting long term signals. A golden cross occurs when a short term moving average crosses a long-term moving average (that is the short-term moving average goes above the long-term moving average). Swing traders will watch the 200-days moving average and 50-day moving average. The golden cross will happen when the 50-days moving average crosses and goes above the 200-days moving average. This is a bullish signal. You want to enter a long position when the 50-days average goes above your 200 days moving average.

f. Death Cross

The opposite type of golden crossing is called a death cross. In that case, the 50-day moving average drops below the 200 days moving average. This is a signal the stock is going to enter a downward trend. So this is a bearish signal, and the 50-day moving average crossing to move below the 200 days moving average either means you should sell your position if you are long or if you are bearish then you'll want to short the stock or buy puts.

Note:

When looking at golden and death crosses, check trading volume. High trading volume is a data point that supports what the cross is telling you. Always confirm a golden cross or death cross with other trading signals. While they are quite reliable, golden and death crosses often lead to false signals.

Jim Douglas

Chapter 8:
Making a Trading plan

a. Analyze your situation

If you are a new trader, you are likely wondering how you buy or sell a security. Whenever the market is open, there are always at least 2 prices listed for any stock or other financial instrument being traded. There is a "bid" and an "ask". A bid is what buying traders are offering to pay for that stock at that particular moment. The ask is the price that traders are wanting in order to sell. A bid is always lower because buyers want to pay less. The ask is always higher because sellers want more for their holding. The difference between the bidding price and the asking price is called the "spread".

These spreads in the bid and ask can vary for each stock and even for the same stock at different times of the day. If the stock does not have a lot of buyers and sellers, then the spread could be quite large (up to $0.50 or more per share). If there are lots of buyers and sellers then the spread between the bid and ask could be as low as $0.01 per share.

When a swing trader wants to enter a position, they have 2 choices. They can pay what the seller is asking immediately or they can place a bid at or below the current bid price. Paying the ask immediately ensures that the order is filled (filled means the purchase transaction is completed). When a trader places a bid at or below the current bid price, they may get a purchase at a lower price. The disadvantage of this purchase option is that the trader may not get their order filled. For example, if a trader puts in a bid to buy an up trending stock, the bid may never get filled, leaving the trader without an entry in a profitable trade.

I will discuss more about entering a trade in Chapter 12, Swing Trading Strategies. An important factor to remember is managing the risk you are taking in each trade and making sure you are not chasing a security price past your planned entry. Managing your risk will be discussed in Chapter 5, Risk and Account Management.

Investment and Margin Accounts

Let's look at 2 types of accounts you can open to trade stocks. One is generally referred to as an investment account and the other is called a margin account. The margin account allows you to borrow against the capital that is in your account. The investment account allows you to buy up to the dollar value you hold in that account. A straight investment account is like a debit card; you cannot spend more than is in your account.

When you open a margin account, you might be at a capacity to borrow money right from your investment organization to enable you to pay for some part of your share or investments. This is referred to "buying on margin". Buying on margin gives you the benefit of being in a position to buy more investments or shares than you would or might be able to manage to pay in comparison to having the basic investment account. This is a way of using or gaining leverage to acquiring greater earnings from your investment. However, it is almost a principle now that with everything that brings greater returns, inevitably also brings along greater risks. When you borrow money to make investments, at some point you need to pay back that loan. Making investments with leverage can magnify the percentage losses on your money.

Here are 9 things you should know about buying on margin:

1. It's a requirement for to open a margin account so as to be able to buy on margin.

2. Investing on margin is generally not allowed in "government registered accounts".

3. The minimum amount to be paid is set by the brokerage firm which must be deposited in a margin account. In other words this is called minimum margin.

4. How much margin you will have access to partially depends on the amount or price of the shares or stocks you're buying (usually stocks that trade under $5.00 are not eligible as margin security).

5. Your investment firm will dictate how much margin they are willing to offer you. Can also be called maximum loan value.

6. Like all loans, there are interest charges applied to any funds you borrow to buy or sell on margin. Those interest costs may be a deduction from your taxable income.

7. The stocks bought are used to stand in for or a collateral for the loan acquired (unless they do not qualify as per point #4) and therefore must remain in your account in order for you to have access to the value of the loan of those securities.

8. If you are at your loan value maximum limit and stocks drop value (assuming you are long), your investing firm will likely get to ask you to bring or put more flow of money in your account to retain your margin. This is referred to as margin call – more on that below.

9. Shorting stocks on margin have different funding requirements versus holding long positions on margin. Check with your broker on their specific funding requirements.

Different brokerages will offer different levels of margin. Some might offer to lend up to 100% of the value of your existing assets in your account. For example, if you hold 100 shares of a security that has a value of $50.00 per share, you have $5,000.00 worth of assets in your account. Therefore, the brokerage firm will allow you access to another $5,000.00 to invest in other securities. Sounds great, but as I mentioned, there is a downside.

If your $50.00 security suddenly drops to $45.00 per share, your broker is going to revise down to $4,500.00 how much they are willing to lend you. If you have already used that $5,000.00 margin to buy another security, you are going to get a call from your broker. This is referred to as a "margin call" and depending on the broker, they may expect you to sell some of the holding immediately to get you back inside of their borrowing requirements.

Alternatively, they could just ask that you immediately put more money into your account to meet their requirements. They also have the right to sell your positions to get your account back in line and they may do this without your approval.

Let's look at an example of shorting on margin. When you short a stock, a broker will want you to maintain a certain amount of excess capital in your account to make sure they do not end up with costs if you do not have enough money to buy back the shares you have borrowed. The usual amount is 150% of the original short value, so if you short shares and get $5,000.00 in your account from selling those shares, the broker will want you to have another $2,500.00 of other shares or dollars in your account as margin.

Imagine that you have the bare minimum when you enter a short. You have $2,500.00 cash and you went short 500 shares at $10.00/share so you have $5,000.00 from the short trade. Your account now holds $7,500.00 of cash and an obligation to replace those shares at a future date. But what if you are wrong and the stock moves against you with the price jumping to $11.00/share – now you immediately need $8,250.00 to maintain that 150% margin requirement (500 shares x $11.00/share = $5,500.00 plus the 50% of $5,500.00 = $2,750.00).

This is when you get the call from the broker to say you need to come up with the extra capital immediately or all or part of the position will be closed. Don't be surprised if the brokerage sells your shares without notice to ensure they do not incur any liability for your short position. It is their right to do so, but with proper risk management and an understanding of this aspect of margin trading, you should not ever get into this situation. Going long and short selling on margin offers an active trader another tool for making money and getting a better return on their investment and can be very effective when combined with some of the strategies in trading that are discussed in this book.

b. Find your objectives

Before I go into the details of how to develop a routine, you should give some thought to the bigger picture regarding your trading business. I encourage you to reflect upon and then write down your responses to the following items:

1. Why am I swing trading? What is my objective or ultimate goal? Is it to build a living around trading or to just manage my money actively so I can save for retirement or for some other purpose? Perhaps it is to build enough income to have a monthly payout that

supplements your existing income. Another possibility is that you are already doing some day trading and you believe swing trading will be a way to improve your trading knowledge, experience and psychology. Decide on your objective or goal for your business and write it down. Post it somewhere that you can easily see it so that it is a constant reminder of your goal. You should also feel free to revisit and modify your goal if your situation, abilities or circumstances change.

2. What markets and securities will I focus on in my business? There are many different investment and trading vehicles that a swing trader can play from cryptocurrencies to individual stocks. All of these options have varying degrees of risk and with this risk comes both reward and the potential for losses. If you are a swing trading beginner, then you should probably start with individual stocks or non-leveraged ETF. If you are a more sophisticated trader, then you may expand on the trading vehicles you are open to working with. Deciding upon what vehicles and markets you will

trade will help you to focus your scans on specific opportunities.

3. Decide on a strategy or set of strategies to use. This decision will be based on personal preferences. Do you want to focus on only long trades, short trades or both? Do you want to focus on only one type of setup such as a double bottom or are you open to more than one of the trading patterns that I discussed in Chapter 9, Technical Analysis – Patterns. These decisions will impact the types of market scans that you perform when searching for trading setups. Once you decide on patterns or trade setups that you intend to use, I recommend new traders write them down and keep them easily accessible for reference. Until you become familiar with your trading strategy, this will help to ensure you are getting the process right.

4. Decide on a stock price range for your trades. If you are starting with a smaller account of $5,000.00 or less you will likely want to focus your trades on lower-priced stocks so you can take a big enough position to

make your trade worthwhile. If you buy 10 shares of a higher-priced stock, it will have to move a lot just to cover the commissions on your trade. Some traders actually focus their attention on trading stocks or securities that are priced under $5.00 per share because they feel that these lower-priced shares give the best potential for gains. The downside of trading stocks under $5.00 per share is that they may not qualify for use as margin in an account, which will limit your borrowing ability and purchasing power. My feeling is that most of the swing trading techniques work on stocks in all price ranges.

5. What time frames are you open to trading? Swing traders normally have some thoughts about how long they want to hold a position. Ultimately, this hold time will depend on how each trade works out and how fast your position hits its target or you get stopped out. Some traders might decide to sell half of a position at a target, move their stop up to stay profitable and keep another half for more gains. This would extend the hold time on your position. A swing trader may also need to modify

their hold time expectations based on the current market conditions. Remember that you can only work with the market you have, you will never win if you try to work with a market that you wish you had.

Once you have the answers to the aforementioned questions and goals, you can start to build a trading routine that you should follow as consistently as possible.

c. Make the trading plan

Trade Management

This section should be empty since you'll be starting off with a set and forget management plan. Once you're past the 200-trade mark, you can look to add your plans in here.

An example might be scaling out of your position once the trade moves past the 2R mark. How much will you scale out? Will you add to your position? Under what conditions? And so on...

As a beginner, you shouldn't worry about all this. Focus on executing the set and forget perfectly and maintaining your mindset on an even keel.

Post Trade Execution

List out the things you will do once your SL or TP is hit. You could run some mental routines, like visualizing yourself as a successful trader or you could just list out the physical actions you will carry out like journaling and taking screenshots.

Beliefs

List out all the correct beliefs about the market here and read them daily to reinforce them in your mind. Whenever you find yourself behaving contrary to these beliefs, remind yourself of these correct ones and you'll soon find that your old, incorrect beliefs are deactivated.

Examples of the correct beliefs could be, "The result of the next trade is irrelevant since I understand how odds play themselves out." Write them in your own words and emphasize what you learned in the chapter where we looked at the mindset necessary for success in the markets.

Learning Plan

A trading plan is all well and good but it assumes you already have certain things in place like knowing which indicators and techniques you wish to use. This section will give you a clear and concise path to getting to a place where you can implement your trading plan.

First Steps

The first step would obviously be reading this book and grasping the philosophy of what is written in here. You may not understand every single detail but that's OK. As long as you grasp that your mindset is the most important barometer of your success and that the majority of your time should be spent on getting the correct mindset in place. There is a reason the majority of this book is about order flow, risk management and mindset. These are what's important. The indicators, etc. are derivatives which make interpreting things easier.

Simulation and Demo

Once you understand this, ideally you should get yourself simulation software like Forex Tester or some equivalent. These software enable you to play the market over, bar by bar, helping you effectively observe them real time. They do cost money but they are the best investment you will make for your trading success.

If this is not an option, for whatever reason, sign up for a demo account with a broker and observe the markets there. Scroll back in time and start observing order flow characteristics as were discussed in the first few chapters. Practice determining whether an environment is trending or ranging. If trending, how strong is the trend? What is the level of balance in the environment?

During your designated trading hours, sit and watch the market unfold real time and determine what environment it is currently in. During these live sessions, observe one or maybe two instruments at a time. If the action is too slow for you, practice by looking at previous bars back in time. The objective is to build your skill set to a level where, upon being presented with a price chart, you can immediately get a gauge of how the buyers and sellers are distributed.

Learning Your Patterns

Next, play around with candlestick patterns and correlate them to the underlying order flow. You can also play around with the indicators discussed here at the same time. Resist the temptation of exploring more indicators because you will just be wasting your time. Any excess energy you have is better directed at observing order flow and getting to know your patterns better, trying to figure out what it is you're the most comfortable with.

Once you can immediately identify your chosen patterns or indicator entry points on a chart, it is time to start placing demo orders. That's right, we're still not live as yet.

Paper and Demo Trading

Once fully comfortable with your chosen technical process, you can start paper trading. Paper trading is simply scrolling back in time and entering trades on paper to see if they would have had a desirable result. As such, this isn't the most efficient way of spending your time.

If you have a simulation software, trading those sessions will give you a real feel of how the markets flow. The software will record your results and your aim is not profit but to get comfortable executing your strategy to the point where you don't second guess yourself and your entry and exit points are clear to you immediately.

It is at this point that you fill out your trading plan and begin demo trading. Your demo trading hours will be the same as your market hours and this will simulate live trading. Execute your demo trades as perfectly as you can and treat it like live trading. Perform your weekly reviews and carry out everything in the most serious manner possible since this is how you will trade live.

Live Trading

Once you're past the 100 trade mark and if you've made money (doesn't matter how much), you're ready to go live! This is when you will open an account with a broker and execute live trades just as you did on the demo platform.

If you haven't made a profit as yet, do not be disheartened! This is not something to worry about. Instead, keep working on your skills and keep analyzing how you can get better. Once you turn a profit for 100 trades (on a rolling basis), you are ready to go live.

Adding Instruments

While you will start off with two instruments, you should not restrict yourself to just that number. You simply rinse and repeat this process with every new instrument right from the order flow stage wherein you observe the rhythms of that instrument.

You then simulate it and then demo trade it. Once you've made a profit over 100 trades, you trade it live.

It is in this scientific way, you build your trading account and your profits. All these actions you perform add up to a sum much greater than their individual parts and over time, you will scarcely believe how much money you're making via trading. However, it all starts with that first step. Make sure it is the correct one.

The Right Market

In both two market limits, the bear grandstand condition or fuming purchaser promote, swing trading exhibits to be an ideally extraordinary test over in a market that is between these two cutoff points. In these limits, also the most powerful stocks won't demonstrate the equal all over movements as when documents are commonly unfaltering for a large portion of a month or even months. The bear market or emphatically slanting business part, vitality will overall pass on stocks/shares for a huge parcel of time one path just, along these lines avowing the best system is to do trade dependent on the more expanded term directional example.

The swing dealer, thusly, is best arranged when the markets are working no spot – when records go up for a few days, by then diminishing for the accompanying couple of days, just to repeat a comparable general model and yet again. A few months may go with noteworthy stocks and documents by and large at a comparative spot as their interesting levels, anyway the swing vendor has gotten various opportunities to get the transient improvements all finished (every so often inside a channel). Clearly, the issue with both the swing trading and the whole deal example trading remains that accomplishment relies upon viably perceiving what sort of market that is correct and now currently being experienced.

The Right Stocks for Swing Trading

The chief key to productive swing trading is picking the right stocks. The best contenders are tremendous top stocks, which are among the most adequately traded stocks on the huge exchanges. In a working business part, these stocks will swing between broadly portrayed high and low breaking points, and the swing dealer will ride the wave one route for a few days or weeks just to change in actuality side of the trade when the stock pivots heading.

Exponential Average Movement

Essential moving midpoints (SMAs) offer assistance and deterrent levels, similarly as bearish and bullish models. Sponsorship and the resistance levels can hail either to buy stock. Bearish and bullish half and half models sign worth centers where you are supposed to enter and leave the stocks.

Exponential moving ordinary (EMA) is an assortment of SMA that spots more stress on the newest data centers. The EMA offers sellers clear example hint and area and leave concentrates faster than an essential moving typical. The EMA half and half can also be used effectively in swing trading to the time section and leave centers.

Basic EMA half and half system can be in use by focusing right on the 9-, 13-and 50-duration EMAs. Bullish half and half happen when the worth traverses these moving midpoints resulting to being underneath. This indicates a reversal might probably work out and an upswing may begin. Exactly when the 9-time period EMA traverses the 13-time span EMA, it banners a long section. Regardless, the 13-time allotment EMA must be over the 50-time allotment EMA or even cross above it. Alternatively, a bearish cross breed happens when the expense of the security falls underneath the EMAs. This banner a possible reversal of an example, and it might be used to stage or track an exit of the long position. Exactly when the 9-time span EMA crosses underneath the 13-time allotment EMA, it banners a short segment or the exit of the long position. Regardless, the 13-time period EMA needs to underneath the 50-time span of EMA or cross underneath it.

Taking Profits

When it comes time to take benefits, the swing trader should leave the trade as close as possible to the upper or lower channel line without being exorbitantly careful, which may cause the threat of missing the most obvious opportunity. In a strong market when a stock is showing a strong directional example, dealers can sit tight for the channel line to be come to before taking their advantage, anyway in a progressively delicate market, they may take their advantages before the line is hit if the heading changes and the line does not get hit on that particular swing.

Baseline

A lot of research on recorded data has shown that, in a potential market accommodating for swing trading, and liquid stocks will by and large trade up and above and underneath a benchmark regard, which is displayed on a graph using an EM). When the swing shipper has tested the EMA to perceive the normal measure on top the stock diagram, the person being referred to move long at the standard when the shares or stock is going up and always up and also short at the benchmark when the shares at stock is going down. Thusly, swing representatives are not planning to smash the amazing pummel with a lone trade – they actually are not stressed over the ideal time to engage and buy a stock unequivocally at its base and sell correctly at its topmost or a different way. In an ideal trading condition, they believe that the stock will hit its example and avow its heading before they even make their moves. These story gets progressively tangled when a more grounded rise or down ward trend is affecting everything: the seller may endlessly go long during those times when the stock dives underneath the EMA and trust that the stock will return up an upswing, or the individual might short a stock up that has injured over the EMA and sit tight for it to go down and drop if the more drawn out example is down.

Swing exchanging is extremely a champion among the ideal trading classes for the start trader to get their feet wet, anyway in any case it offers basic advantage potential for moderate and pushed vendors. Swing sellers get sufficient analysis on the traders trades following a number of days to maintain and keep them animated, yet their mostly long and short places of a couple of days that are of the term that actually does not instant redirection.

Swing Trading is a framework that spotlights on taking more diminutive gains in transient examples and cutting hardships quicker. The increments might be smaller, yet done dependably after some time they can compound into extraordinary yearly returns. Swing Trading positions are ordinarily held a few days to half a month, anyway can be held longer.

Swing Trading Strategy

We should begin with the essentials of a swing exchanging system. As opposed to focusing on 30% to 45% benefits for the majority of your stocks, the benefit objective is a progressively humble 20%, or even only 10% in harder markets. Those kinds of increases probably will not appear to be the extraordinary rewards ordinarily looked for in the securities exchange, however this is the place the opportunity consider comes. The swing dealer's attention is no on increases creating over weeks or months; the normal length of an exchange is progressively similar to 5 to 10 days. Along these lines, you can make a great deal of little successes, which will indicate huge in general returns. In the event that you are content with a 20% increase over a month or more, 5% to 10% increases each week or two can mean huge benefits.

Obviously, regardless you need to factor in misfortunes. Littler additions can possibly create development in your portfolio if misfortunes are kept little. Instead of the typical 7% to 8% stop misfortune, take misfortunes faster at a limit of 2% to 3%. This will keep you at a 3-to-1 benefit to-misfortune proportion, a sound portfolio the executive's rule for progress. It's a basic segment of the entire framework since an outsized misfortune can rapidly wipe away a great deal of advancement made with littler additions. Swing exchanging can even now convey bigger gains on individual exchanges. A stock may display enough introductory quality that it tends to be held for a greater increase, or incomplete benefits can be taken while giving the rest of the position space to run.

Take breakouts from solidifications. Earlier upswings are an absolute necessity. Sideways activity that opposes surrendering much ground is liked. High Relative Strength Ratings are a key measurement for constraining your universe to the best prospects. What's more, volume gives you affirmation that foundations are aggregating shares. The wind included by swing exchanging is the time period.

As opposed to unions that are normally five to seven weeks at any rate, you may take a gander at a large portion of that time or even less.

The adaptability in taking a gander at shorter time periods originates from brought down benefit objectives. An earlier upswing of 30% or all the more needs the more extended time span of a sound base structure before proceeding for comparative measured gains or better. Yet, on the off chance that you are searching for an increase of 5% to 10%, the necessities are considerably less.

By a similar token, volume qualities of a breakout additionally can have an abbreviated time period. Instead of the 50-day moving normal of volume as your edge for overwhelming turnover, look to the volume of the shorter union territory for pieces of information. On the off chance that the breakout volume can outperform the ongoing movement, that can be an adequate affirmation of solidarity.

Jim Douglas

Chapter 9:
Some Strategies to Maximize Short-Term Trading

Day traders rely on four basic strategies to make daily profits in the stock market. Let's review each of them.

Scalping

Chances are you're familiar with the concept of scalping tickets to an upcoming event, maybe a music concert or high demand sporting event. The idea is you buy the tickets at face value, then when it's sold out you show up at the venue and offer your tickets for sale at a premium price to make a profit.

Scaling isn't the same on the stock market, but scalping is the most basic strategy used by day traders. At its core is the notion of "buy low, sell high". When a day trader uses scalping, they buy the shares at a given price, and then sell immediately when they stand to make a profit. So, if you buy 100 shares of ABC company for $10 a share, a total investment of $10 x 100 = $1,000, you then closely monitor the share price to sell when it becomes profitable. Suppose that at first, it drops to $9.50 a share, and bounces around a bit. Then it jumps up to $11.75 a share. At this point you'll sell right away, earning:

100 shares x $11.75/share = $1,175

Since you invested $1,000 to buy the shares, you've made a quick profit of $175. Scalping is a good way to get your feet wet with day trading, it's a very basic strategy. Of course, you're not going to get into scalping on a random basis, you're going to want to study the markets, keeping up with financial news, and choosing companies that are likely to show an increase in share price that day. This illustrates that day trading is not something you can do while at work or while going out to play golf. You must take an active role in the markets in order to make it work on a systematic basis. Sure, you could buy some stock before heading to the office, and maybe you get lucky and check at lunch and the price is higher so you can sell at a profit. But often, the price may have gone up into a profitable range and may have either dropped down so your profit is a lot less than what it could have been or you're even in a losing position. Scalping isn't very complicated, but it does require that you stay on top of the markets to increase your odds of success and to maximize your success if it does arrive.

Scalping is a pretty basic concept, and that isn't really day trading (although you can certainly do it). Day trading involves planning ahead using well thought out strategies. The first strategy that we'll look at involves using pivot points.

Daily Pivot

The stock market is very volatile, in some sense being guided by chaotic randomness as prices rise and fall at the whims of large numbers of buyers and sellers. Of course, the volatility isn't entirely random, and over the long-term, it gets smoothed out. However, the day trader attempts to take short term advantage of that volatility.

Daily pivot is a strategy that centers on buying your shares at the low point of the day and then (hopefully) selling them at the high point of the day. This strategy does involve a bit of guesswork, there is really no way to know with any certainty what the low and high points of the day are going to be ahead of time – so there is a strong possibility that you will guess wrong.

Of course, we don't want to trade based on a "guess", we're going to use a strategy based on facts (it still may be right or wrong, but we rely on real data to make our trading decisions). This idea is based on the fact that most of the time when dealing with short term movements of stocks, trading is going to proceed based in some part on what the shares have done in the very recent past.

So you calculate what's called a pivot point. This has three inputs: the previous day's high, low, and close. The pivot point is simply the average of the three:

Pivot point = (high + low + close)/3

Now suppose that we have stock for XYZ. The high, low, and close the previous day were $102, $97, and $100. The pivot point is then:

Pivot point = ($102 + $97 + $100)/3 = $99.67

Now to figure out how to proceed with our trades the following day, we will calculate some support points and points. We will explain what the means in a moment, but first let's learn how to calculate the support points.

Support point 1 = (pivot point x 2) – high from the previous day

Support point 2 = Pivot point – (high – low)

Our support points in this case would be:

S1 = ($99.67 x 2) - $102 = $97.33

S2 = ($99.67) – (102 - $97) = $94.67

Next, we need two resistance points. The formulas used for these are:

R1 = (pivot point x 2) – low from previous day

R2 = Pivot Point + (high – low)

For our example the resistance points are:

R1 = ($99.67 x 2) - $97 = $102.34

R2 = $99.67 + ($102 - $97) = $104.67

We see that the resistance points are above the pivot point, with R1 being a little bit above, and R2 being the most above the pivot point. The support points are below the pivot point, with S1 being a little bit below, and S2 being the lowest point. The numbers R1, R2, S1, S2, and P are only valid for one trading day. Each trading day you need to calculate them using the previous days trading data, prior to the stock market open. You can find pivot point trading calculators on Google.

Stop loss points

A stop loss is a point that is chosen as a kind of insurance to limit losses incurred on security. This is done with a stop-loss order. What you do is you place an order with the broker to buy or sell the stock when it reaches a certain price. As an example, suppose you buy XYZ stock at $100. After you purchase the shares, you can place a stop-loss order for $95. What this does is your shares will be sold if the price drops to $95. That protects you from incurring even more losses if the stock is tanking.

The buy signal

The point of doing these calculations is to determine when to buy, when to sell, and when to cut your losses. The buy signal occurs when the price of the stock goes above the pivot point with conviction. You are bullish on the stock, expecting the price to keep rising (it may not). Your first profit target is given by R1.

By conviction, that means that the stock price is moving up fast. The volume also figures in when evaluating conviction, more volume means more conviction. If there are a lot of volumes and the price is moving up fast, that means more buyers are bullish on the stock.

For our case, the pivot point was $99.67. If the price breaks strongly above this, we take that as a buy signal. The previous days close was $100 so we will say for this example that the share price jumped to $101. We could decide to buy the shares at this price.

The profit point is R1, which is $102.34 based on our calculations. You could choose to sell if the stock price hits R1. However, if the stock is rising rapidly, then you can choose R2 as your profit target. In that case, you would wait until the price hits $104.67 to sell.

If you are right, then you purchased shares of XYZ stock at $101 per share. If we buy 100 shares, then we are in for:

100 x $101 = $10,100

Now suppose that it does hit R2. We immediately sell, so our gross revenue is:

100 x $104.67 = $10,467

We've made a profit of $10,467 - $10,100 = $367. If that was the only trade, we made that day, then we've made a pretty nice daily income of $367.

Of course, things don't always go as planned, which is why you need a stop loss point. You do this so that you can minimize losses and avoid losing your shirt. Whether you stick to R1 or R2 as the point at which you'll sell for a profit or not will depend on how rapidly the stock is going up. So, you'll be looking at a measure of its momentum. The stop loss points S1 and S2 correspond to each case. For R1, which is $102.34, your stop loss point would be S1 = $97.33. If the stock is shooting up and immediately goes above R1, you can take P as your stop loss. If it has gone up to R1 but doesn't show more conviction (i.e. that it's going to go up to R2) then you sell at about R1 and take the smaller profits.

If you are shorting a stock as described in the previous section, then the roles of the Rx and Sx points reverse, with R1 & R2 playing the role of stop loss points and S1 and S2 representing profits.

When to use pivot points

There is no solid agreement on this. Some traders believe that pivot points are at their highest accuracy right after the market opens, and so they believe you should utilize them within the first hour of trading. Others believe that the first half-hour of the trading day will have too much volatility, so you should wait before using them.

Morning or Opening Gaps

A morning gap is when a stock opens higher or lower than it closed the previous day. Suppose that XYZ stock closed at $50. If it opens the next morning it opens at $51, then this would be a $1 gap up. On the other hand, if the stock opened at $49.50, that would be a 50-cent gap down.

A strategy that day traders use is called fade the gap. There are two options:

• If the stock opens up, take a short position.

• If the stock opens down, take a long position.

The bet while using this strategy is that the stock is going to return to a value near the previous days close. This is called filling the gap. In other words, you're betting on the opposite trend the stock had at the opening of the markets.

With options trading:

• If the stock opens up, you'll buy puts on the stock.

• If the stock opens down, you'll buy calls on the stock.

Jim Douglas

Conclusion

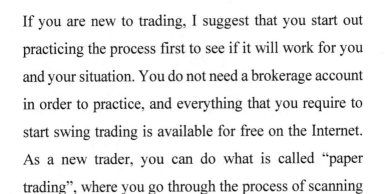

If you are new to trading, I suggest that you start out practicing the process first to see if it will work for you and your situation. You do not need a brokerage account in order to practice, and everything that you require to start swing trading is available for free on the Internet. As a new trader, you can do what is called "paper trading", where you go through the process of scanning for trades, identify opportunities and pretend to enter the trade. Start with an imaginary account size that is the same as you intend to begin with if you do take the next step and trade with real money. Try to keep your simulation as realistic as possible in every respect.

Journal your trades as you would with a real trade and see how they work out. If you find you enjoy the process and think it will work for you, then you can consider opening a brokerage account and putting your real capital at risk. Be aware that many traders say that it becomes a little more difficult when they switch from simulated or pretend accounts to trading with real money. This is because you are not as emotionally attached to your play money compared to your real money. Once emotions get added to the mix, trading can become more difficult. For the more experienced traders, you will likely already know many of the concepts and principles set forth in this book. I hope that there was still enough new information to help you find and make more profitable swing trades.

Regardless of your level of experience, a swing trader gets to slow everything down, and that is an advantage, especially for new traders. You do not get caught up in a process where you need to make a decision in a matter of seconds. This type of pressure situation is where many day traders lose out and let their emotions get the better of them. Swing traders have the luxury of time to make their decisions and are less likely to make an impulsive trade move in the heat of the moment.

Regardless, all of us have mental weaknesses that we must overcome as traders.

As a disciplined trader, you will do your scans of the charts, recognize patterns and develop trading strategies. You will make a plan and stick with it unless something fundamentally changes with the reasons you entered the trade. And that can happen. You should stay in tune with the market and be aware that you might need to adjust your trading strategies as the market sentiment changes. You must also accept that there is no shame in losing on a trade. Not all trades will go in your favor. You need to accept that and move on. If you do not follow your trading plan when the trade does not work out, then you will likely pay the price in your account. Some traders are unwilling to accept a loss and exit stocks that trade against them. Others will take small profits early instead of waiting for their planned profit target. These are the actions of a trader who will struggle to make gains.

Last but not least, if you enjoyed reading this book and found it useful, I would very much appreciate if you took a few minutes to write a review on the Amazon website. The success of a book like this is based on honest reviews, and I will consider your comments in making revisions. If you have any feedback, feel free to send us an email.

The information contained in this book is only a suggested starting point for doing additional independent research in order to allow you to form your own opinions regarding trading and investments. Investors and traders should always consult with their licensed financial advisors and tax advisors to determine the suitability of any investment.

Thank you for reading, and happy trading!